Alcohol
Home Detoxification
and Assessment

Alcohol
Home Detoxification
and Assessment

David B Cooper RMN, FETC

Foreword by Douglas Cameron

RADCLIFFE MEDICAL PRESS • OXFORD and NEW YORK

A catalogue record for this book is available from the British Library

ISBN 1 85775 060 8

Typeset by AMA Graphics Ltd., Preston
Printed and Bound in Great Britain by
T. J. Press (Padstow) Ltd, Padstow, Cornwall

Dedicated to my wife Jo without whose love, faith and encouragement what follows would never have been, and to Phil, Marc and Caroline for their understanding and support. Also in memory of Rose Harvey (7 May 1993).

Acknowledgements

I am grateful to Dr Tim Stockwell for kind permission allowing reproduction of some measurement tools used in this paper.

A special thank you to Tim Stockwell, Ian MacEwan, Jim Murphy, Doug Cameron and Jo, for the time spent reading, advising and commenting on this paper, for which I am truly grateful. Any errors, omissions or deficiencies within these pages are the sole responsibility of the author.

Note

Never presume that the home detoxification procedure is understood. It is essential to check that the client and family understand the procedure and what is expected of them. They also need to know what they can expect from you and other agencies involved, at each contact. Always avoid the use of jargon; it can easily be misunderstood.

Abbreviations used in this book

ARP	alcohol related problem
ATU	alcohol treatment unit
BAC	blood alcohol concentration
BP	blood pressure
CAF	continuing assessment form
CAS	community alcohol service
CAT	community alcohol team
CNS	central nervous system
CPR	cardiopulmonary resuscitation
DTs	delirium tremens
FBC	full blood count
GP	general practitioner
HD	home detoxification
HDP	home detoxification procedure
HEA	home environment assessment
IAF	initial assessment form
LFT	liver function test
P	pulse
PI	problems inventory
RMO	responsible medical officer
SADQ	severity of alcohol dependence questionnaire
SSA	symtom severity assessment
SSC	symptom severity checklist
T	temperature
WHO	World Health Organization

Contents

Foreword

Those of us who have been part of the movement over the past 25 years, towards deinstitutionalization of the management of people with drinking problems, have been aware of an apparent contradiction.

In-patient units caring for problem drinkers had amassed considerable skill and knowledge in the medical management of alcohol withdrawl states and had minimized the very real risks of mortality and morbidity related to these states. Yet we knew that large numbers of drinkers had found ways of managing their own withdrawal problems where they normally lived, whether that be at home, in a hostel or on the street; and that they succeeded without medical assistance. What should be the role of community-based care for problem drinkers? Could we let our patients/clients simply get on with 'drying themselves out' as they had done before, or did we need to admit them to hospital for detoxification before instituting community care. Of course, we did both.

There was also a third alternative, which was to export from hospitals the expertise that had to be developed there and to administer it 'at home'. The use of 'home detoxification' enables us to avoid episodes of in-patient care, with its inherent high costs and secondary problems of label attachment and possible stigmatization.

This book provides practical advice and guidance on home detoxification from a nursing perspective. If all the procedures outlined here are followed, the care worker of whatever discipline is unlikely to encounter major difficulties. Rather like learning to drive a car, the task at first looks daunting as there is a lot to do and remember, but many of the questionnaires and procedures are no more than common sense. They could well become a model of the kind of comprehensive assessment and structured intervention that is increasingly required as we move towards community care of people with a whole range of conditions.

When asked what community care meant, somebody cynically replied, 'care by the nearest female relative!'. There is more than a grain of truth in that; and when undertaking a home detoxification it is well to remember that we professionals do not really do it. We simply offer support and expertise to other, informal carers and to the drinkers themselves. Establishing a meaningful alliance with them is mandatory: home detoxification cannot be imposed upon those who do not want to give it a try. But for those who do, this book should enable professionals to organize the process with confidence.

DOUGLAS CAMERON
Senior Lecturer in Substance Misuse
University of Leicester

1 Introduction and background to home detoxification

The term 'detoxification' can be applied in several ways. It can be used to imply a 'process' whereby a substance leaves the body, ie removal of alcohol or a poison; or it can refer to an 'action', ie a treatment which entails subjecting oneself or another person to a 'process'.

Within the caring professions, alcohol detoxification is largely still recognized as a treatment. What follows aims to examine and explain this method of treatment.

Dr Tim Stockwell[1] developed the currently recognized model for home detoxification, which he defined as:

'a treatment designed to control both medical and psychological complications which may occur temporarily after a period of heavy and sustained alcohol use.'

This book will use Dr Stockwell's model throughout.

Withdrawal from even small amounts of alcohol consumption will have physical effects as the substance decreases within the body. These may be relatively minor, such as sensitivity to light, irritability or thirst. Only a small proportion of people with alcohol related problems will have withdrawal symptoms that are so severe that they risk experiencing delirium tremens (DTs) or convulsions.

Most people withdrawing from alcohol do not require medication or intensive supervision; whilst the presenting symptoms may be uncomfortable, they are clearly not dangerous. In such instances, supervision by the general practitioner (GP) or other trained support staff is adequate.

For those who do experience marked withdrawal symptoms, one could argue for effective, safe and humane management for the withdrawal syndrome. Stockwell[1] stresses that treatment for alcohol withdrawal should be an essential component of every integrated community alcohol team (CAT).*

Thus it is clear that severe alcohol withdrawal does require a specific medical response.

The symptoms of alcohol withdrawal occur when the blood alcohol concentration (BAC) drops, causing the body to react as the drug decreases. The central nervous system (CNS) then becomes excited and activity is increased as alcohol's depressant effects wear off. The Royal College of Psychiatrists[3] put forward the following analogy that describes the consequences of alcohol withdrawal and its effect on the body.

'The processes that have countered depression of brain activity in the presence of alcohol cause a surge of excitation when alcohol is removed. The analogy might be with the door that has a person on one side pushing it, and on the other side someone holding it shut . . . suddenly stop holding it shut, and the pushing of the person now sends the door flying open with great energy.'

Blood alcohol concentration being at its lowest after a period of sustained abstinence, symptoms experienced, for example, on waking from a period of sleep are good indicators of the severity of the client's dependence[†] on alcohol. Table 1 shows the three distinct factors associated with the alcohol withdrawal syndrome, identified by Gross et al.[5]

---

*Community alcohol teams are a specialist NHS service. Staffing usually consists of a nurse(s), social worker(s) and administrator. Some teams also include other professionals, eg a probation officer, health education officer, occupational therapist, psychologist or doctor. A CAT may have a consultant psychiatrist directly attached or a consultant with a specialist interest in substance abuse attached on a sessional basis. The teams offer counselling, help, advice, information, health promotion, home detoxifications and some specialist therapies[2]. They are sometimes referred to as alcohol advisory services.

†Dependence can be divided into two areas, either or both of which may or may not be present when the individual presents with a drinking problem. These areas have been defined by the World Health Organization (WHO) as follows. 'Psychic dependence—a condition in which a drug produces a feeling of satisfaction and a psychic drive that requires periodic or continuous administration of the drug to produce pleasure or avoid discomfort.' 'Physical dependence—an adaptive state that manifests itself by intense physical disturbances, ie the withdrawal or abstinence syndromes, made up of specific arrays of symptoms and signs of a psychic and physical nature that are characteristic for each drug type[4].'

Table 1.1   Principle factors associated with alcohol withdrawal syndrome

1 Physiological and psychological signs including:

- mood disturbance
- panic
- tremor
- nausea
- sleep disturbance

- anxiety
- sweating
- increasing fearfulness
- muscle pain

2 Distortion of perception and hallucinations (visual, audio and tactile).
Related symptoms include nausea, muscle pain and sleep disturbance

3 Confusion, disorientation and disturbance of consciousness

Whilst anxiety is a common complaint in withdrawal after mild and severe alcohol dependency, the intensity often varies between individuals. The client who is experiencing a mild withdrawal syndrome may complain of craving, mild tremor and some general discomfort. However, the individual experiencing a severe withdrawal syndrome may complain of day and night sweating, marked tremor, strong craving, itching, nausea, panic attacks and fear of the dark.

Some problem drinkers[†] require intensive treatment to regulate these withdrawal symptoms, thus preventing severe psychological and physiological consequences. Uncontrolled detoxification should be avoided at all costs as this can lead to potentially life-threatening problems for the client.

However, there is not, nor should there be, a rigid approach to alcohol withdrawal. Any treatment intervention offered should depend upon the identified needs of each client, which should follow a full and systematic assessment. Edwards[7] suggests that the clinical significance of alcohol withdrawal often lies in the demands it places:

'. . . on the clinician to see the different needs of different patients, and to manage minor withdrawal states without unnecessary fuss, while at the same time learning to recognize the necessity for great care in treating potentially dangerous situations.'

[†]The term 'problem drinker' includes all problems, eg physical, psychological or social, experienced by an individual as a consequence of his or her alcohol use/misuse. This does not necessarily require tolerance or physiological or psychological dependence on the drug[6].

Clients' fear of home detoxification

Fear of the unknown may often prevent the client from initially agreeing to undertake detoxification within the home. However, he or she is more likely to agree to this approach to care than to hospitalization. Stockwell et al.[8], found that most clients treated in their study stated that they would have been unwilling to accept in-patient admission for detoxification.

It is important to stress to any potential client that detoxification can be safely undertaken at home with very little fuss or problems, and to offer reassurance that full and active support will continue throughout. Unnecessary admissions to hospital, that lead to the invalidism of the client and excessive time off work, should be avoided as much as possible.

Detoxification by non-medically trained personnel

Home detoxification can be monitored by fully trained, non-medically qualified personnel, such as social workers, probation officers or voluntary counsellors. However, it is advised that a thorough assessment of the client's likely withdrawal symptoms be undertaken by a nurse specialist or specifically trained medical practitioner. An agreement must be reached between all parties involved that enables the nurse specialist to support the carer appointed throughout the detoxification process.

The supervisory carer must have clear and effective links with the client's GP, who should be willing to ensure that any medication is correctly and adequately supplied. The latter should be directly accessible at all times in case he or she is needed. Primary links and agreed levels of supervision and support should be established with the nurse specialist, before detoxification commences if appropriate.

Withdrawal in the treatment context

Therapeutic intervention commences, in reality, at the first engagement in any structured change process, and continues throughout the change. This book specifically refers to one form of therapeutic intervention as part of the process of alcohol withdrawal management.

Withdrawal management is part of a broad-based treatment and counselling package offered to the client. To change/modify one's drinking behaviour does not necessarily require detoxification. However, in those who do require detoxification, withdrawal is only the start of the recovery process (regardless of the chosen outcome), and as such should not be considered to be the only intervention required. Once withdrawal is completed, clients may continue to require additional interventions for some time, at varying levels according to individual needs.

Assessments should look beyond detoxification and prepare for future, additional and appropriate interventions which may come to light as developing needs dictate. There is little point in arranging home or in-patient detoxification if it is not required. Neither procedure should be regarded as a routine to be undertaken in every case involving alcohol withdrawal.

The home detoxification process should involve a structured and mutual partnership between carer and client. It is not enough that the nurse or other professional supervising the detoxification feels the individual should undergo intensive treatment. The client must also have a clear understanding of what is expected, as well as a desire to participate, if the outcome is to be successful.

Some GPs prescribe medication without a clear regime; they neglect to undertake a full assessment which enables agreement on the desired needs of the individual involved and the anticipated treatment outcome. The consequences of such action can be far reaching and may lead to dependence on the prescribed medication in addition to the existing alcohol dependency problem. Often the only advice given to the client is that he or she should stop drinking; this is clearly not enough.

Case study

The following highlights two common problems experienced by problem drinkers: first, the problem of staff attitudes in relation to in-patient detoxification; second, the consequences of repeat prescriptions and the effect these have on those with drink related problems.

Jane was a single, 29-year-old woman. She had been admitted to the acute admission ward of a large mental health unit on five previous occasions. The ward was always very busy and disturbed during her admissions and that usually meant that the nursing staff had very little time for her. Some nurses had strong negative views about 'alcoholics' who took up much needed beds: didn't they always 'come in and out, they never changed'.

Jane's admissions for detoxification always followed the same pattern. She would feel low and lonely and would start drinking heavily, usually vodka. Eventually she would go to her GP complaining of depression. In the past he had prescribed lorazepam and diazepam. On the last occasion he had prescribed nitrazepam and chlormethiazole, to 'help' her while she stopped drinking. On each occasion preceding her admission, Jane would drink large amounts of alcohol, then overdose on her prescribed medication. On three occasions she had nearly succeeded in taking her own life.

All the above drugs were prescribed repeatedly. This information was never made available to the hospital. Neither were they aware that Jane was dependent on all of them, and especially on lorazepam and nitrazepam.

Following each overdose, Jane was transferred from the general hospital to the mental health unit. She would feel isolated there, having little in common with her fellow patients and finding the environment noisy and harsh. Jane would often go for walks on her own and some staff took this as an indication that she was hiding something and therefore 'she must be drinking'. Jane would be asked where she had been and whether she had been drinking. Each time she would be warned about the ward policy, ie that if any patient was caught drinking alcohol, all 'alcoholics' would be discharged.

The duration of Jane's admissions usually depended on how long she could put up with such accusations. Eventually, unable to stand any more, she would discharge herself. This vindicated the staff view that she must have been secretly drinking: 'after all, aren't they all like that'.

On the last occasion (the sixth), Jane's admission to the mental health unit was refused and she returned home. Around the same time, another GP took over her practice. He had heard of a new CAT in the district and asked them for help.

Jane was detoxified at home, with a nurse specialist visiting three times daily and contact being made as required through a special number. The GP and the nurse specialist both remained in close contact. An exceptional amount of work followed, involving all three participants; as the level of dependence became clear, each substance was dealt with one at a time.

Throughout the 18-month detoxification (in Jane's case detoxification was very much an extended process because of the combination of drugs misused and the cautious need for a slow, structured and extended detoxification process) Jane had just one brief relapse of three days. This preceded an interview for a disulfiram implant. After two implants, Jane no longer required this support or the subsequently prescribed oral disulfiram. For three years the nurse specialist continued to visit once a week for counselling. Jane progressed well.

The case was much more involved than this outline. However, the above gives some indication of what is achievable if close co-operation exists between the nurse specialist and the client's GP. It also highlights the problems that many people with alcohol related problems experience in their encounters with the caring professions.

Home detoxification and work commitments

In some cases it is not practical for the client to continue working whilst undergoing the home detoxification treatment process. However, this decision should be based on individual need and circumstances and must not form part of a standard procedure.

One should always enquire if the client can arrange for annual leave or an extended weekend leave during the early stages of home detoxification. Alternatively, a brief period of self-certification may be required. This very much depends on the individual and on his or her ability to cope with some uncomfortable symptoms of withdrawal during the first few days of detoxification. The security of home and family support may be needed, as anxiety levels will be at their highest at this stage.

When to commence detoxification

It is vital for the success of home detoxification that it is commenced at a time convenient to the client. It would be morally and ethically[§] wrong to insist that detoxification starts on a particular day of the week to suit the nurse specialist or the service purchasers/providers.

If possible, try to arrange additional support for the client, eg from an alcohol advisory service, community alcohol team, other support groups or Alcoholics Anonymous. In addition, one should not forget the support required by the family, whose needs at this time will require careful consideration and detailed attention. In most cases, the spouse will do the majority of the supervision and caring during detoxification; his or her role cannot be over emphasized and will be addressed in more detail later.

[§]Ethics: a code of moral principle. Nursing ethics: the code governing a nurse's behaviour with patients and their relatives and colleagues[9].

Doubts

If there is any doubt about the suitability of the client for home detoxification, it is appropriate to arrange for a brief hospital admission of two or three days. This allows for assessment of any potential problems. The client can be discharged and detoxification continued at home if minimal physiological problems are experienced. Conversely, if home detoxification fails, then consideration should be given to hospital admission.

Complications of withdrawal

In order to minimize complications in the withdrawal process, one should maintain a careful balance between the physiological and psychological care offered to the client. Grand mal seizures (withdrawal fits) are most likely to occur 24–96 hours after cessation. However, it is important to note that these can also occur up to six weeks post-withdrawal.

Wernicke's encephalopathy and Korsakoff's amnesic state

It is estimated that at least 60% of people with severe alcohol problems are vitamin deficient[10,11]. Poor nutrition, impaired absorption (caused by gastritis, liver damage, vomiting or diarrhoea) and an increase in metabolic demand (eg when alcohol oxidizes during drinking and withdrawal) can cause deficiencies in vitamin B complex. This includes B_1—thiamine, B_6—pyridoxine and C—ascorbic acid.

A deficiency in thiamine may lead to the development of Wernicke's encephalopathy[12], the symptoms of which are outlined in Table 1.2. It is therefore important to provide prophylactic intervention in the form of vitamin replacement as soon as a risk is identified. However, one must also remember that the symptoms outlined may not always be present in a person with vitamin deficiency.

Table 1.2 Symptoms of Wernicke's encephalopathy

- peripheral neuropathy
- confusion
- blurred vision
- stupor
- unsteady gait or ataxia
- external ocular palsies
- unco-ordinated eye movement

Whilst Wernicke's encephalopathy is treatable and the symptoms are reversible, subsequent progression to Korsakoff's amnesic state[12] is a potential long-term problem if thiamine deficiency remains untreated. The key symptoms of this are failure to lay down (or properly to retrieve) recent memories in a person in clear consciousness, and a tendency to confabulation[13]. Such damage, when established, is irreversible and thiamine or other vitamins administered at this stage have no effect.

However, it is important to stress that alcohol misuse is not the only factor for consideration in vitamin deficiency in the problem drinker. There are strong indications that the client's social environment and circumstances sometimes play an integral part in its development. These factors should be fully assessed and accurately interpreted prior to detoxification.

Alcohol withdrawal states

Alcohol withdrawal can produce a wide range of physical and psychological symptoms which vary in severity between individuals. Table 1.3 outlines some of the more severe symptoms sometimes experienced during uncontrolled withdrawal. As these are also symptomatic of other diseases, such as pneumonia, head injury or liver failure, it is important to rule out these possible causes[7].

Symptoms of alcohol withdrawal states may commence whilst the client is still drinking or on cessation. Onset can be slow or, conversely, explosive in nature.

Table 1.3 Signs and symptoms of severe alcohol withdrawal

- fear
- hallucinations
- agitation
- delirium
- delusions
- restlessness
- heightened suggestibility
- tremor
- physical disturbances: sweating
  dehydration
  poor appetite
  increased blood pressure
  fever

Table 1.4 Selective severity assessment (SSA) scale

▪ eating disturbances	▪ sleep disturbances
▪ agitation	▪ hallucinations
▪ tremor	▪ perspiration
▪ clouding of consciousness	▪ temperature
▪ pulse	▪ convulsions
▪ quality of contact	

The main indicator that the client may develop alcohol withdrawal problems is a history of excessive and frequent alcohol consumption over a sustained period.

The symptom severity checklist (SSC)[14], was specifically designed for use during alcohol withdrawal and will alert the nurse specialist to any potential problems during the monitoring of alcohol detoxification. An alternative assessment tool is the selective severity assessment (SSA) scale[15], from which the SSC was developed. This was specifically designed to look at the areas outlined in Table 1.4.

It is imperative to remember that an estimated 10–15% of people attempting to 'give up' die in alcohol withdrawal states; the more severe the dependency, the greater the risk of death[13]. Thus, careful assessment and interpretation is essential.

Delirium tremens

Edwards[7] described the main indicator of the onset of delirium tremens (DTs) as vivid visual hallucinations (eg crawling spiders) which often present as bad dreams. Delirium tremens usually commence 24–48 hours following cessation of alcohol. A very high BAC for several days before an abrupt withdrawal may precipitate the onset. These symptoms can last 3–5 days, with the intensity varying between individuals.

Other withdrawal problems

Additional problems that can be associated with alcohol withdrawal include:

▪ craving—usually decreases over 10–15 days
▪ acute anxiety
▪ depressed mood—usually improves after 2–6 weeks
▪ general discomfort—eg irritability, boredom.

Relapse

It is perhaps important to add a further note of caution at this point. All of the complications outlined can also be considered as contributing factors in potential client relapse, and as such they require specific assessment, observation and appropriate attention.

Relapse and some causative factors are discussed in greater detail in Chapter 15. However, one cannot over-emphasize the importance of the client's and his or her family's understanding of the relapse processes, and what can and should be done in such an eventuality, particularly in terms of seeking help and support.

Alcoholic hepatitis and liver damage

Alcoholic hepatitis

This usually occurs in cases of a prolonged history of heavy and sustained alcohol abuse. The onset can be sudden and dramatic, with a mortality rate of 10% during the attack: the liver becomes acutely inflamed and liver cells die. An early indication of alcoholic hepatitis may come from liver function tests, which will give abnormal results with high bilirubin and enzyme levels. Table 1.5 lists the signs and symptoms of acute alcoholic hepatitis.

Liver damage (cirrhosis)

If the problem drinker continues to drink alcohol, then he or she may develop liver cirrhosis. Symptoms include an enlarged and firm liver, sometimes with a rough surface, and an enlarged spleen owing to the liver's resistance to the flow of blood from the portal vein. The problem drinker may also develop signs of portal hypertension. Table 1.6 outlines the signs and symptoms of liver damage. As with all such cases, the client will require hospitalization and appropriate medical attention.

Table 1.5 Signs and symptoms of acute alcoholic hepatitis

- patient quickly becomes ill
- fever
- jaundice
- abdominal pain
- enlarged tender liver
- hepatoma
- signs of hepatic encephalopathy

Table 1.6 Signs and symptoms of liver damage

Early stages
- non-specific digestive disturbance
- anorexia
- flatulence
- nausea
- loss of weight
- morning retching
- diarrhoea
- enlarged liver

Intermediate stages
- jaundice
- dependent oedema
- spider angioma
- anaemia
- increased abdominal girth

Advanced stages
- splenomegaly
- neurological involvement (hepatic coma)
- haemorrhage from oesophageal varices

Assessment tools in home detoxification

Assessment tools always have their critics. Choice of tool is often a matter of personal preference and comfort of use for the client in view of his or her individual needs. Some experts argue that, as the chance of success and the severity of withdrawal symptoms are dependent on the quantity and frequency of the individual's alcohol intake, it is unnecessary to measure dependency with assessment tools such as the severity of alcohol dependence questionnaire (SADQ)[13]. Others would suggest that the SADQ must be an integral part of the home detoxification assessment process[16].

The symptom severity checklist (SSC)[14] suggested for use within these guidelines will alert the nurse specialist to the onset and severity of withdrawal symptoms. The selective severity assessment (SSA) scale designed by Gross[15] may usefully fulfil the same task in home detoxification assessment.

I would suggest that you try out various assessment tools to find the ones that work best in personal practice, that you feel comfortable with, and that are easiest for you to interpret and understand. The assessment tools used in this guide are those employed in Dr Tim Stockwell's study[1] and by the author when a practitioner. The nurse specialist undertaking the home detoxification assessment may prefer an alternative. However, it should be stressed that assessment tools are not a substitute for sound clinical judgment. It is important that all tools used to aid assessment in alcohol withdrawal have been competently researched and appraised in controlled clinical practice prior to general use.

References

1. Stockwell T (1987) The Exeter home detoxification project. In: Stockwell T and Clement S (eds) *Helping the problem drinker: a new initiative in community care*. Croom Helm, London.

2. Cooper DB (1993) The range of therapeutic facilities. In: Wright H and Giddey G (eds) *Mental health nursing: from first principles to professional practice*. Chapman and Hall, London.

3. Royal College of Psychiatrists (1979) *Alcohol and alcoholism: report of a special committee of the Royal College of Psychiatrists*. Tavistock, London.

4. World Health Organization (1974) 20th report of the WHO expert committee on drug dependence. WHO, Geneva.

5. Gross MM, Lewis E and Hastey J (1974) Acute alcohol withdrawal syndrome. In: Kissin B and Begleiter H (eds) *Biology of alcoholism. 3: clinical pathology*, pp 191–263. Plenum, New York.

6. Cooper, DB (in press) People with dependency problems. In: Alexander M, Fawcett T and Runciman P (eds) *Nursing practice: hospital and home—the adult*. Churchill Livingstone, Edinburgh.

7. Edwards G (1987) *The treatment of drinking problems—a guide for the helping professions*. 2nd edition. Blackwell Scientific Publications, Oxford.

8. Stockwell T, Bolt L, Milner I *et al.* (1990) Home detoxification for problem drinkers: acceptability to clients, relatives and general practitioners, and outcome after 60 days. *British Journal of Addiction*, **85** (1), 61–70.

9. Weller, BF and Wells RJ (1990) *Baillière's nurses' dictionary*. 21st edition. Baillière Tindall, London.

10. Majumdar SK, Shaw GK and Thomson AD (1981) Blood vitamin status in chronic alcoholics after a single dose of polyvitamin: a preliminary report. *Postgraduate Medical Journal*, 57, 164–6.

11. Shaw GK and Thomson AD (1977) A joint psychiatric and medical out-patient clinic for alcoholics. In: Edwards G and Grant M (eds) *Alcoholism: new knowledge and new responses*, pp 328–34. Croom Helm, London.

12. Vortmeyer AO (1993) Wernicke's encephalopathy, Korsakoff's amnesic state and thiamine deficient encephalopathy (letter to the editor). *Alcohol and Alcoholism*, 28 (2), 199–200.

13. Cameron D (1993) Personal communication.

14. Murphy DJ, Shaw GK and Clark I (1983) Tiapride and chlormethiazole in alcohol withdrawal: a double blind trial. *Alcohol and Alcoholism*, 18 (3), 227–37.

15. Gross MM, Lewis E and Nagarajan M (1973) An improved quantitative system for assessing acute alcoholic psychoses and related states (TSA and SSA). In: Gross MM (ed) *Alcohol intoxication and withdrawal: experimental studies*. Plenum, New York.

16. Stockwell T, Murphy D and Hodgson R (1983) The severity of alcohol dependence questionnaire: its use, reliability and validity. *British Journal of Addiction*, 78 (2), 145–55.

2 Advantages of home detoxification

There are many advantages of home detoxification for both the client and the service provider. There are financial benefits, which are covered in greater detail in Chapters 6 and 7, and personal benefits for the client, discussed in this chapter.

Home detoxification ensures that the client can remain within, and make full use of, the home and family support network. It enhances the continuing care process during the involvement of the primary worker and the nurse specialist.

Avoidance of hospital admission reduces the risk of stigma associated with in-patient mental health care. It is also desirable in cases where clients have unpleasant experience of past admissions. Many clients are unlikely to accept in-patient treatment; they feel more secure at home. However, there is a need for careful screening for suitability for home detoxification. Withdrawal and the use of prescribed (and non-prescribed) medication must be closely monitored.

Most importantly, home detoxification enables the family, and others affected by the client's drinking, both to give support and be supported. Full advantage should be taken of this situation by seeking active involvement in the detoxification process.

Problems associated with hospital admission

Hospital environments are rarely appropriate to the needs of the individual with alcohol related problems (ARPs). The two key factors are ward environment and staff attitude.

Ward environment

All wards are busy areas: admissions, discharges, patient movement, and the coming and going of doctors, nurses and other ward staff can all present difficulties. Such constant activity is a problem when one is feeling unwell and in need of a quiet safe environment. General hospital wards tend to have structured regimes which offer patients little freedom of movement and severely restrict the activities they can undertake. The problem drinker, in most cases, will not be 'ill' in the same sense as other patients on the ward, and generally will not require intensive nursing care in addition to the observation outlined herein. Trained nursing staff on such wards are, especially in the present economic climate, a scarce commodity.

Even if the nurse has the time, it is unlikely that she will possess the skills required to counsel the problem drinker. Therefore, these patients are often left for long periods without active therapy/inter-vention or any stimulus. Meanwhile, they have to deal with the occupants of nearby beds, who will want to know the reason for admission. Even disregarding this, hospital wards are not the best places for confidentiality. The increasing trend of nursing 'hand over' taking place at the foot of the bed, no matter how quietly one talks, cannot assist in protecting the patient's confidentiality—closing the curtains round the bed does *not* block out sound.

The mental health unit presents similar problems. Nursing time is often taken up with clients with severe mental health problems, and occupational therapy too is geared to meet the needs of such clients rather than those of the individual withdrawing from alcohol. The question of whether somebody with a drinking problem is mentally ill is much debated.

Mental health units have a greater stigma attached to them than the general hospital ward: how does one explain the admission to a mental health unit to one's employer? The health care professions still like to label and categorize the individual, and the label is recorded in the notes. As a consequence, other physical and psychological problems are often overlooked; they are put down to 'the drink', so are not properly investigated.

Staff attitudes

The attitudes of staff towards patients with a drinking problem can interfere with the outcome of treatment. The retort that problems resulting from drink or drug misuse are the client's own fault is not uncommon. Some health care professionals have expressed the opinion that problem drinkers deny 'much worthier patients' nursing care. Revolving door admissions act to reinforce these stereotype views. The case studies in Chapter 1 (page 5) and below outline common problems. Some details have been changed to protect the individuals concerned. One would wish that these were rare occurrences, but regrettably this is not yet the case. Both cases demonstrate real problems experienced by problem drinkers in hospital. The admissions were in different health districts.

Case study

Roger was a 37-year-old businessman who led a very active business and social life. Work often included long lunches, where many a good deal was clinched after not a little help from alcohol. In the evening Roger liked to unwind with a drink or two before dinner, and always drank wine with his meal. His wife did not like wine much, so Roger would often finish off the bottle.

Most days ended with an evening at the local pub with friends; sometimes his wife would go with him. Roger always arranged for his wife or a friend to bring him home, as he did not drink and drive, although he did not mind if the friend had had a drink. 'It's a free choice', he would reason, 'and it's his licence, not mine'.

Roger found it increasingly difficult to sleep, and suffered from indigestion and heartburn. His GP prescribed sleeping tablets and antacid medication, but these did not seem to help.

Roger could no longer cope with his business commitments; he was often late for or missed important appointments, and he lost a lot of custom.

Roger turned increasingly to drink to help him get through the day. Eventually his GP referred him to the local hospital for detoxification. Roger could not identify with his fellow patients: 'After all', he thought, 'you can see that they are ill'. He also felt that the staff did not like him. He was angry and bitter, and did not always feel like socializing, unsurprisingly because he had lost a lot, and felt frightened and degraded in hospital.

The ward staff were always busy. Roger felt they resented him because he took up too much time being awkward when they wanted him to do anything. He just wanted peace and quiet: 'Can't they see that?'. He needed to think; this admission would not help his business—how would his creditors feel if they knew? He wanted to talk but no-one seemed to have the time. Some senior staff, who had seen many such detoxifications, were convinced that Roger was secretly drinking and had accused him on several occasions. This made Roger angry: 'Is this really worth it?' he thought.

Finally, unable to cope with his feelings about being in 'this place', Roger discharged himself.

In the above case, the behaviour of the ward staff instilled defiance in Roger and he has remained 'dry'. For others, however, their hospital experience has been a precipitating factor to relapse. Thus the door continues to revolve, and existing staff beliefs are reinforced[1].

Reference

1. Cooper DB and Faugier J (1993) Substance misuse. In: Wright H and Giddey M (eds) *Mental health nursing: from first principles to professional practice*. Chapman and Hall, London.

3 Disadvantages of home detoxification

The disadvantages of home detoxification need to be actively considered in each case. The home environment may contain an excessive number of 'triggers': it could be that alcohol consumption normally takes place at home, with family or friends; access to alcohol may be easy. Therefore, external pressures on the problem drinker may be strong, with the immediate 'rewards' from drinking outweighing the long-term benefits of abstention or moderation.

Hospital admission can offer short-term avoidance of these 'triggers'. This technique is occasionally used in behavioural management, but long-term survival requires more active coping skills.

Several studies have stressed the value of family support in successful treatment outcomes for this client group. However, existing problems within the family (eg marital problems) may lead to additional stress during detoxification. The husband may want to re-establish control of his family, for example in the management of discipline and/or financial matters. He may try to compensate for lost time with the children by lavishing attention on them and trying to be the model father. The spouse, however, may not want to relinquish this control, having fought long and hard to gain it against the odds. She may not wish to take the risk that her husband will destroy it all again. Thus, the conflict of roles may prompt the need for 'time out', allowing separate therapeutic intervention for each partner and a 'cooling off' period. In such situations, short-term hospital admission may be appropriate if there is no other suitable alternative.

There are many dangers associated with unsupervised home detoxification, especially if the client has access to prescribed medication and alcohol. Excessive use of medication and access to repeat prescriptions are a potentially lethal hazard. Clients are often tempted to increase medication to alleviate withdrawal symptoms. Therefore, it is unrealistic to expect self-monitoring of prescribed drugs.

Self-administration of drugs can produce over-reliance and increases the temptation to avoid reducing medication when this is appropriate. Overdose or long-term dependence on other substances, and poly-drug abuse, are also potential problems. In all cases it is recommended that external observation and monitoring of drug use, with mutual agreement on adjustments, be regarded as the norm in home detoxification.

4 How many problem drinkers?

All estimates of the total number of problem drinkers tend, by their nature, to be conservative. However, some statistics are very useful for statutory bodies.

The total cost to the NHS of alcohol related problems (ARPs) was £149.35 million in 1990[1]. £26.51 million went into in-patient mental health units, while £109.41 million went into other forms of psychiatric intervention for ARPs. It is estimated that 200 000 life-years are lost per year due to alcohol related problems, with an overall cost to the nation of approximately £2.5 billion[2].

It is currently estimated that each health district has, on average, 43 000 people who currently drink more than the recommended sensible limit[3]. Approximately 13 750 problem drinkers in each district are presently in contact with the caring professions as a consequence of their alcohol misuse.

Twenty per cent of beds in acute mental health units are occupied by people with a diagnosis of alcohol dependence. Often such admissions are unnecessary and excessively long, being solely for detoxification[4].

The author[5], looked at levels of alcohol consumption in clients admitted to a 25-bed acute admission ward (mental health) over a three month period, excluding those with a diagnosis of ARPs. The survey indicated that 38% of respondents drank in excess of the so-called 'sensible limit' put forward by the Royal Colleges. In none of these cases had the issue of alcohol consumption, and its possible role in the individual's mental health problem, been fully explored.

It has long been acknowledged that a community response facilitates contact with people with identified ARPs and builds their confidence in seeking help. Care within the home environment allows for closer contact, especially with those who habitually fail to keep out-patient appointments. The non-attendance rate at out-patient clinics, of clients with alcohol related problems, has been estimated at 50%.

As one researcher after another produces data supporting the theory that alcohol related problems exist and need to be addressed, health districts still pour money into research. Each district appears to want its own proof. Is this a delaying tactic or avoidance of reality? Are we not just putting back the day when we must respond positively to this problem?

If there is any need for further research, it is to answer two questions. First, do clients feel that community care is better for them? Second, how much money is being wasted on unnecessary and costly in-patient care for problem drinkers?

Financial comparisons have been made and cost savings highlighting the effectiveness of community care have been identified. Unfortunately, the extra money generated by these savings has not been spent on appropriate and far reaching intervention and prevention work. Even if 50% of such savings were transferred to community alcohol teams, a substantial improvement in early identification, and consequent reduction of additional costs, would be achievable.

There appears to be a fundamental belief that senior executives know best how to spend monies saved. Moreover, faced with all the factual information from decades of research, managers still tend to ask 'What do the experts know?', and to demand local proof. This is clearly unnecessary and a waste of valuable time and much needed resources which could be utilized elsewhere.

References

1. Maynard A (1992) *Social costs of alcohol: is it helpful to measure social costs of alcohol use?* Research and training information, Yorkshire addictions research, training and information consortium.

2. Alcohol Concern (1993) *Response to the White Paper 'The health of the nation'*. Alcohol Concern, London.

3. Personal communication (1993) Alcohol Concern information office, London.

4. Tait J (1986) Responding to alcohol. Speech to a national symposium, Manchester.

5. Cooper DB (1983) *Alcohol consumption of admissions to an acute mental health unit*. Unpublished internal report. Faringdon Wing, Luton and Dunstable Hospital.

5 Home detoxification: some statistics

Information on the number of home detoxifications undertaken in each health district is available from several sources. How successful such a service provision is very much depends on the motivation of staff, on effective publicity saying what such a provision has to offer, and on ease of access to that provision. These issues are addressed in Chapter 17.

This chapter looks at three health districts that introduced a home detoxification service, and reviews some of the first year results. The health districts were:

1 Blackburn, Hyndburn and Ribble Valley, 1984–5.
2 Forth Valley, Scotland, 1991–2.
3 North East Essex, 1988–9.

Blackburn

Blackburn, Hyndburn and Ribble Valley Health Authority had no specialist service provision for problem drinkers before the introduction of home detoxification and a community alcohol service (CAS). The population in the district was 275 000.

The health district was divided into three, all areas having a similar population mix. The service split was as follows: Ribble Valley had no service provision at all; Hyndburn received, on request, advice only in relation to alcohol related problems; Blackburn, an industrial town which also encompasses some outlying rural areas, received a full research-based CAS, offering treatment, prevention, education/training, health promotion and home detoxification. The approximate population served by a home detoxification facility was 92 000 (Blackburn).

During the first year (1984–5) 171 referrals were received from the input area (Blackburn), indicating a mean 3.3 home detoxifications per week. If these figures are projected to cover the entire district, one could estimate a referral rate of 513 per annum, a mean of 9.9 home detoxifications per week. One third of clients participating in home detoxification were female[1].

Forth Valley

Research undertaken by Colin Bennie, Clinical Nurse Specialist (addictions) in the Forth Valley, was commenced in 1991 and was due for completion at the end of March, 1993. Forth Valley health district incorporates large rural and urban areas and had no home detoxification programme prior to its introduction during Mr Bennie's research. The population offered this service was 273 000[2].

For the 10-month period to November 1991, a total of 300 home detoxifications were carried out, a mean of 5.8 per week. Of those detoxified at home, 26% were female[2,3].

North East Essex

North East Essex, which covers urban and rural areas, initially undertook detoxification on an in-patient basis. Of those treated within the acute mental health unit, 12% eventually participated in a structured, total abstinence in-patient programme within the alcohol treatment unit (ATU). In 1988 the ATU closed and a community-based service, offering treatment, prevention, education/training, health promotion and home detoxification, replaced it. The population offered home detoxification was 250 000.

During the year 1988–9, 235 referrals for home detoxification assessment were received by the team; 83% ($N = 195$) of these detoxifications were undertaken in the client's home, a mean of 3.75 per week. Twenty-six per cent of those detoxified at home were female.

In-patient detoxifications accounted for 9% ($N = 22$), a mean of 1.8 per month[4]. However, it may be argued that with experience, and as the service develops, this level of in-patient detoxification will

Table 5.1 In-patient detoxification: reasons for admission

1 admission preferable (not specified)
2 home environment not suitable
3 previous withdrawal problems warranted admission
4 questioned motivation
5 client/GP refused home detoxification

decrease. The reasons for hospital admission could be categorized into five areas, which are listed in Table 5.1.

During the study period, the nurse specialist was called upon to give indirect advice and support to GPs and other professionals. These indirect home detoxifications accounted for 8% ($N = 18$), a mean of 1.5 per month[4]. Whilst direct supervision was not given, it is important to note that this is a developing, additional and vital role for the nurse specialist, which will continue to expand as demands on the service increase. As such, it is a time-consuming but worthwhile and recognizable part of the nurse specialist's role.

References

1. Cooper DB (1985) *The effects of a community alcohol service, the hidden 'potential drinking problems' and problem drinking.* Report to the district management team, Blackburn, Hyndburn and Ribble Valley Health Authority.

2. Bennie C (1992) Home detoxification for problem drinkers: a pilot study. In: *Alcoholism,* No 1, the quarterly newsletter of the Medical Council on Alcoholism.

3. Bennie C (1991) *Home detoxification service for problem drinkers.* Report for Forth Valley Health Authority (personal communication).

4. Cooper DB (1989) *Community alcohol services—North East Essex.* Paper presented at a national conference on prevention and intervention for problem drinkers. Essex University, Colchester.

6 Counting the cost of in-patient care

Cooper[1,2,3] suggests that clients admitted to acute mental health units for detoxification remain in hospital for unnecessary and prolonged periods of time, and questions the benefits of such admissions, therapeutically and financially.

Most clients with ARPs feel insecure in hospital. The essential needs for peace, quiet and counselling often go unnoticed in such a busy environment. In some wards suspicion of this client group is such that they are often asked to prove that consumption has not taken place. Any attempt to seek solitude results in the assumption that 'they must be hiding something'.

Clients may feel threatened and unable to identify with others. Ward-based occupational therapy does not appear to meet their needs. The feeling that nothing is being done can quickly lead to relapse and self discharge.

Prolonged admissions lead to 'cocooning' from external problems and pressures. Thus, when clients are discharged, they may be unable to cope with any new crises, and existing problems appear unsurmountable. These may then contribute to a further relapse.

Those clients who do re-present for admission, receive little sympathy; staff make such entrenched comments as 'He is always in and out', 'She will never change' and 'Alcoholics are all the same'—the door continues to revolve.

In any case, hospital admission is an expensive alternative to home detoxification, especially in terms of treatment outcome, relapse and financial stresses on limited NHS resources.

A three-month bed occupancy study was undertaken during 1988, covering two acute mental health admission wards. One or more beds were occupied for 88% of the survey period by clients with ARPs who required detoxification; the mean bed occupancy was three such clients per day[2]. These results were comparable to an earlier study of bed occupancy by problem drinkers in an acute mental health unit[4].

Throughout the survey, 26 clients with ARPs were admitted, of which 73% were readmissions. The duration of in-patient care ranged from one to 43 days, a mean of 12 days per client[2].

Only 12% of all ARPs admitted to hospital were referred to the newly established community alcohol team during or following discharge (at the time this service did not offer a home detoxification service). On further investigation, there appeared to be no justification for such a low referral rate other than it 'had not been thought of' by the carers already involved as a post-discharge care option.

In terms of financial implication for the district health authority, a total of 308 days (in three months) accounted for in-patient care of ARPs[2]. At an estimated cost of £178 per day per client (1993 prices), the total cost for three months' care is £54 824 (a mean treatment cost per client of £2108.62).

The gross annual treatment cost based on these figures amounts to £219 296. This sum would be sufficient to set up and run a home detoxification service with one nurse specialist and support staff for three years. Additional savings are automatically made because one nurse specialist is capable of treating at least two to three times the number of clients with ARPs each day, than can be treated in hospital.

It does not take a financial expert to maximize use of savings involved by introducing home detoxification, by investing in improvements to community alcohol services or voluntary alcohol advisory services.

District health authorities that have introduced a home detoxification service report that bed occupancy by clients with ARPs has substantially decreased following the introduction of community alcohol teams coupled with a home detoxification facility. However, primary access to this client group remains by way of the GP (as an alternative to hospital admission), as opposed to there being an internal uptake of such services; the latter is often slow and requires continual reinforcement[5].

References

1. Cooper DB (1985) *The effects of a community alcohol service, the hidden 'potential drinking problems' and problem drinking*. Report to the district management team, Blackburn, Hyndburn and Ribble Valley Health Authority.

2. Cooper DB (1988) *Ward population survey: alcohol related bed occupancy*. Report to the Assistant General Manager, North East Essex Health Authority, Mental Health Division.

3. Cooper DB (1992) *An holistic approach to problem drinking in East Suffolk: home detoxification and Suffolk Community Alcohol Service*. A joint funding proposal.

4. Cooper DB (1984) *Ward population survey: alcohol related problems and bed occupancy*. Report to Blackburn, Hyndburn and Ribble Valley Health Authority.

5. Cooper DB (1989) *Community alcohol services—North East Essex*. Paper presented at a national symposium on alcohol misuse. Essex University, Colchester.

7 Example costing for one nurse specialist

Good public relations and quality communication are of paramount importance when establishing a home detoxification service; there are no short cuts.

Effective publicity materials must be made available to all service users, concurrently with face to face contact and effective feedback. Whilst time consuming and initially costly during the setting up period, this method has proven financially beneficial in the long term. In the business world of today's health services, self-promotion and communication are the keys to success, as business people in the private sector have demonstrated. Thus, public relations activities form an integral component of any home detoxification service provision, and must continue to do so. Special training events will need to be organized to facilitate appropriate service take-up and this is reflected in the costing detailed below[1,2].

The cost of clinical supervision has been deliberately excluded. How much supervision is required depends on the level of competence of the nurse (one would suggest that a salary graded 'H' would attract a nurse with a high degree of clinical competence, who could operate as an independent practitioner), and whether in-house expertise is available (supervision must otherwise be purchased from an external source). It is recommended that a level of supervision is agreed and made available to the nurse specialist, from a nurse who is already competent in home detoxification techniques and alcohol related issues facing the problem drinker. Daily administration and general management will depend on the organizational structure. The GP remains the responsible medical officer (RMO).

The costing in Table 7.1 makes the assumption that the service commences from a 'zero' resource point, is adequately research-based (as all home detoxification and community alcohol/drug teams should be) and includes secretarial/research assistant support.

Table 7.1 Home detoxification: service costing (one nurse plus support)

Expenditure	Yr 1	Yr 2	Yr 3
Nurse 'H' Grade inc psychiatric lead	23 221	25 543	28 097
Oncosts 12%	2787	3065	3372
Lease of car (3 yr)	3300	3630	3993
Petrol for 20 000 miles at (est) 50p per mile	1650	1815	1997
Secretary/research assistant—			
18½ hrs per week	4220	4642	5106
Oncosts 12%	506	557	613
Joint training budget	1300	1430	1573
Total employment costs	**36 984**	**40 682**	**44 751**
Insurance/management/accommodation	15 000	16 500	18 150
Computer/program	3000	200	220
Desk/chair/file	2000		
Ansaphone/fax/photocopier	2000	100	110
Lion breathalyzer	500	10	11
Thermometer	13		
Digital sphygmomanometer	150		
Needles/syringes/urine bottles	300	330	363
Stationery/printing	3000	1650	1815
Training events/materials	1300	1430	1573
Total collective costs	**64 247**	**60 902**	**66 993**

The total funding for a three year project stands at £192 142. The figures allow for a 10% increase in costs per annum. However, it may be possible to charge for training events, so this avenue of funding should be fully explored. It has been estimated elsewhere that the total cost of a home detoxification service may represent as little as 26% of the equivalent cost for in-patient care for problem drinkers[3].

The nurse specialist's salary has been estimated at 'top point' of the current (1993) nursing 'H' grade, and makes the assumption that one wishes to employ (and keep) a highly skilled nurse, who has considerable experience in research as an independent practitioner within the substance misuse field.

The inclusion of a nurse training budget allows for current UK Central Council (UKCC) re-registration requirements and the eventual introduction of post-registration education and practice (PREP). Additional monies have been added to fund 'networking' at a national, regional and local level, which must be actively encouraged if the nurse specialist is to maintain his or her level of expertise and introduce new developments into the service.

The annual figure of £64 247 p.a. (1993), to fund one community nurse specialist undertaking home detoxification, represents 29.2% of the total annual cost for in-patient care (£219 296[2] as mentioned on page 28). As well as being cost effective, home detoxification can give three to four times the number of clients active therapeutic care and interventions than in-patient provision.

References

1. Cooper DB (1985) *The effects of a community alcohol service, the hidden 'potential drinking problems' and problem drinking.* Report to the district management team, Blackburn, Hyndburn and Ribble Valley Health Authority.

2. Cooper DB (1992) *An holistic approach to problem drinking in East Suffolk: home detoxification and Suffolk Community Alcohol Service.* A joint funding proposal.

3. Stockwell T, Bolt L, Milner I *et al.* (1991) Home detoxification from alcohol: its safety and efficiency in comparison with in-patient care. *Alcohol and Alcoholism,* **26** (5/6), 645–50.

8 Assessing suitability and establishing need

The assessment of suitability and level of supervision required for home detoxification must be undertaken by a trained nurse or other appropriate medically trained personnel. The final decision to proceed cannot be delegated and *must* rest with the individual who will undertake the detoxification supervision, following full consultation.

Stockwell[1] suggests that *all* assessments should answer two specific points to ascertain whether there is a need for supervised home detoxification.

1 Is there a need for any medication to alleviate withdrawal symptoms?
2 Are there any reasons for *not* keeping the client within the home environment for detoxification?

In the process of establishing a need for home detoxification, it is imperative that there is no 'hard sell' approach to this option by the nurse specialist.

The client who has, over a period of several weeks, consistently expressed a desire to stop drinking alcohol altogether, and who has only minor withdrawal symptoms, may not need intensive supervision or medication. However, the individual whose consumption is heavy and has been continuous up to the day of assessment, will require careful assessment, intensive monitoring and supervision, especially if there is a possibility of other drug use.

It has been suggested that, as a 'rule of thumb', medication is unlikely to be required for women drinking less than 12 units of alcohol per day and men drinking less than 16 units per day[1]. If consumption exceeds 30 units per day, a decreasing dose of medication will be required as routine during withdrawal. As there is no absolute dividing line, clients should be assessed on their individual needs, and decisions relating to the requirement of medication taken accordingly.

If a client is using tranquillizers or other CNS depressants, the combination of these drugs with alcohol will increase the severity and duration of withdrawal symptoms. Therefore, it is important that, in addition to the recent drinking history, other drug use should be fully explored, including prescribed, over-the-counter, and any other legal or illegal drug use.

The client who experiences withdrawal symptoms as the BAC drops, eg on waking, and immediately drinks alcohol for relief of the symptoms, will need medication. Another useful indicator is the reporting of experiences during previous attempts to abstain from, or control, alcohol use.

Reference

1. Stockwell T (1987) The Exeter home detoxification project. In: Stockwell T and Clement S (eds) *Helping the problem drinker: a new initiative in community care*. Croom Helm, London.

9 Assessment of risk and factors to look for when screening

A problem drinker with a history of withdrawal fits or DTs is not suitable for home detoxification. Caution is required when looking for early indicators of possible DTs, such as hearing voices, seeing objects or feeling sensations (eg crawling). Always check with the GP to see if he or she has any knowledge of these or any other psychological or physiological reasons why home detoxification should not take place. Remember that it is not possible, regardless of how skilled one is, to provide such close supervision within the home, as is available in hospital.

The nurse specialist who supervises the withdrawal must have a clear understanding of how to identify withdrawal symptoms and of the interventions required in the event of severe withdrawal symptoms. If these skills are available, then there should, in most circumstances, be no problem with detoxification within the home.

It is essential that a thorough and careful assessment of the home environment is undertaken when deciding suitability for home detoxification. Table 9.1 lists some of the most important factors to look at.

Table 9.1 Home environment assessment

- Does the home environment allow for some privacy and quiet?
- Is the home overcrowded?
- Are supportive and co-operative relatives, friends or neighbours available to help the client?
- What are the alcohol and drug use of the family or friends?
- Has, or will, all alcohol be removed from the premises? An explanation of why this is required should be given, ensuring that the consent form is signed once agreement has been reached.

Warning signs

Warning signs that the detoxification process is not going as planned, or that home detoxification should not take place, may include:

- severe diarrhoea especially if accompanied by increase in fluid loss from sweating or vomiting
- increase in pulse
- decrease in blood pressure
- hypothermia
- decrease in level of consciousness which continues even when medication is withheld.

10 Rapid response

A rapid response to referrals is an integral and imperative part of any home detoxification facility (or indeed any substance misuse service provision). It is important to act quickly and offer positive intervention whilst the client is actively within the change process: 'Strike whilst the iron is hot!'.

Olkin and Lenle[1], whilst looking at out-patient appointments, demonstrated the importance of seeing a client within 48 hours of the initial telephone referral. They suggested that clients seen within this time range are significantly more likely to keep an appointment.

Kennedy and Faugier[2] summed up the importance of offering a rapid response to substance misuse clients as follows:

'Usually, it is a crisis or deterioration that facilitates behaviour change . . . We would not say to a smoker, "Well, this has been a problem for the past 20 years, so why rush for help now?". Yet, it rolls very smoothly off the tongue when addressed to the drug user or problem drinker'.

There can be no such thing as a waiting list for those who are experiencing substance related problems. Delays do influence treatment outcome and they are avoidable with a little thought, planning and careful organization.

Offering a rapid response is also a key 'selling point' for potential service providers/purchasers and, perhaps more importantly, service users; and to offer a 24–48 hours response time is a reasonable proposal.

Finally, one could suggest that to make an individual wait for detoxification is to offer a poor quality service leading to the prolongation of health related problems which can only delay good recovery.

References

1. Olkin R and Lenle R (1984) Increasing attendance in an out-patients alcoholism clinic: a comparison of two intake procedures. *Journal of Studies on Alcohol*, **45** (5), 465–8.

2. Kennedy J and Faugier J (1989) *Drug and alcohol dependency nursing*. Heinemann Nursing, Oxford.

11 Family considerations and assessment

What follows is designed to give an overview of family problems requiring consideration during the assessment process for home detoxification. It is not intended to be a definitive statement on the subject and additional reading and knowledge are necessary before one is competent. This chapter merely attempts to emphasize the importance of the family in the assessment process and home detoxification.

Whilst it is accepted that home detoxification is a specific treatment, supervised by the nurse specialist or other component professional, it is essential to remember that the professional's role is one of support and expertise. During home detoxification it is the client who experiences the withdrawal and the family who provide the support and care. The client is in the best position to identify change in his or her withdrawal, and this experience is important because health is often subjectively defined for the individual[1].

Unlike other professionals, nurses work in close and frequent contact with clients and their families[1]. As such, the nurse's fundamental concern must be to attempt to understand and respond to the client and the family's reactions to treatment and care[2]. These social interactions may influence the outcome of any intervention, and the nurse undertaking assessment and supervision of detoxification must always be aware of this[1].

If home detoxification is to come to a successful conclusion, then the nurse must accept that both the client and family are key participants. It is, therefore, essential that they agree to work together to achieve the detoxification goal.

The family may be thrown into a state of turmoil as a result of the intervention, causing disruption to normal family life. It is perhaps useful to remember that people often react in accordance with the sense they make of a given situation[3]. Thus, a full and clear assessment of the family (eg spouse, children and other significant family members) should be undertaken prior to any decision to offer home detoxification, or other therapies or interventions.

Home detoxification places a considerable amount of additional stress on families already in crisis. Moos[4] emphasizes the necessity for a high degree of warmth and support for the family if treatment outcome is to be successful.

The problems faced by the family of a problem drinker are numerous. Alcohol misuse is a known contributing factor in the breakdown of relationships and in child abuse[5,6]. This may not be the first time the drinking partner has promised to control or stop consumption of alcohol, and the spouse will have many doubts, anxieties and questions (Table 11.1). Such established difficulties can present problems in home detoxification, and these require careful discussion and consideration prior to the spouse agreeing to support the problem drinker.

Any change that affects the problem drinker will directly affect the family, and thus they will also be required to make changes. Therefore, the spouse should be assessed as an individual in his or her own right; that is, given an equal opportunity to explore the consequences of the partner's drinking behaviour. Time and encouragement to talk freely and openly is important. Spouses should feel valued and that what they have to say is being listened to and understood.

The spouse

In the past, the spouse will have been forced to make changes that would not normally have been agreed to, and will therefore need

Table 11.1   Doubts and questions which may be raised by spouse of problem drinker

- Does s/he mean it this time?
- Can I trust him/her enough to hand back responsibility?
- Will s/he remain abstinent?
- Can I change?
- How soon should I hand back responsibility?
- Can I accept the 'new' helpful and caring attention?
- Do I resume sexual contact; will it be normal?
- Will s/he still abuse me/the children?
- Will there be less violence?
- Do I really love my partner?
- How and when can I renew my broken social contacts?

support, encouragement and reassurance if the change process is to be entered into therapeutically. How the spouse has adapted to the drinking partner's behaviour, and the numerous problems presented, will vary. The non-drinking partner may adopt various coping strategies during attempts to deal with the consequences of the partner's alcohol misuse and its effects on the family; some of these are outlined in Table 11.2

Edwards[7] suggests that the spouse of the problem drinker may deal with problems presented as a consequence of the partner's alcohol misuse on two levels. The emotional and reality levels he describes are outlined in Table 11.3.

The spouse may proceed through many stages, which can range from an initial reluctance to accept that the partner has a drinking problem, to marital breakdown (Table 11.4). However, it is essential that one remembers that all families are different; some may never experience such problems or may experience entirely different ones.

Table 11.2   Coping strategies which may be used by the spouse of a problem drinker

---

Attack.   Confrontation is used in an attempt to control drinking behaviour. The spouse may threaten to leave, and uses verbal defamation and occasionally physical attacks.

Circumvention.   The spouse withdraws from the problem. Contact with the problem drinker is minimal and basic. Sexual and emotional contact is reduced.

Constructive help seeking.   Information relating to the nature and treatment of drinking problems is collected and studied. Contact with alcohol agencies may be made.

Constructive management.   The spouse adopts the role of family provider. The maintenance of personal dignity is a priority. He or she looks after financial affairs and may take employment to maintain the family status, as well as dealing with the day to day running of the home and its repairs.

Manipulation.   Deliberate attempts are made to embarrass the problem drinker in an attempt to shame him or her into a change in drinking behaviour. This may extend to deliberate drunkenness in order to demonstrate the effect this has on the family. Every opportunity is used to highlight the personal suffering of self or siblings.

Spoiling.   The spouse 'cares' for the problem drinker by cleaning up vomit or urine, comforting when unwell, and preparing meals even if these are refused. Rewards may be offered in exchange for altered drinking behaviour.

Table 11.3 Problems on 'emotional' and 'reality' levels experienced by the spouse of a problem drinker

Emotions	Reality
misery	home loss
fatigue	debts
depression	other financial problems
conflict	loss of employment
loss of value	drinker incontinence
anxiety	violence
fear (for self and children)	quarrels
self doubt/blame	complaints
depravation	jealousy
humiliation	drinker uncleanliness
isolation/loneliness	social estrangement

Table 11.4 Stages experienced by the spouse of a problem drinker

The spouse may go through some or all of the following, not necessarily in this order.

- reluctance to accept partner's drinking problem
- attempts to control/prevent drinking behaviour
- social isolation
- protective strategy (invitations/social occasions refused)
- realization that strategy not working
- drinking problem worsens
- physical/mental health affected (eg depression)
- reduction of sexual contact
- estrangement in relationship
- fear and/or anger
- decides to act
- encourages problem drinker to seek help
- marriage breakup or problem withdrawal

In some rare cases, the partner's drinking problem represents an acceptable part of the spouse's existence, and he or she may even need the element of control that results from the drinking partner's loss of responsibility. However, it must be stressed that such situations are uncommon and are the exception rather than the norm. In such cases, the spouse may deliberately attempt to disrupt the home detoxification.

In other situations, especially if the problem drinker is female, there may be a reluctance to become involved in the home detoxification or to offer any form of support. It is generally accepted that the male spouse is less tolerant and supportive of his partner's drinking behaviour. Some regard the problem as being exclusively that of the problem drinker, whilst others accept that it is a family problem and as such will need to be addressed collectively.

Assessment

Assessment of the family is an integral part of the initial procedure prior to offering home detoxification. However, one should always be aware that observations made by the spouse and problem drinker may be subjective because of their active involvement in the drinking problem. Perhaps the best advice comes from Edwards[7], who said:

'. . . by assessing the coherence of either account and by looking sympathetically at the likely biases, the attempt must be made to arrive at the most accurate possible view of certain important objectives—how damagingly, for instance, this man has really been drinking.'

The spouse should be interviewed in his or her own right and not as an addendum to the problem drinker's assessment. This should be undertaken as a separate interview; afterwards, both parties can be brought together to agree on joint action, and to formulate a care plan.

The assessment format for the non–drinking partner may closely follow that outlined for the drinking partner in Chapter 12.

It is essential that one is cognizant of the fact that the involvement with the family does not cease after the initial assessment. The nurse specialist may need to assist in the process of 'building bridges' and in supporting both partners in adapting to the changes in lifestyle that they will undoubtedly experience as a result of the change to drinking behaviour. Therefore, counselling and other appropriate therapies and interventions should be planned as early as is practical.

Marriage difficulties are not all resolved once detoxification is completed and appropriate referral for marital or family therapy may be appropriate. It may be that professional support during the breakdown and ending of the marriage is needed to make it less painful and destructive than might otherwise be the case.

Children

Children should not be excluded from the problems and decisions made by their parents. Each child will have a particular, and unique, set of problems. Exclusion from the parents' problems can lead to self-blame, loss of self-value and low self-esteem. The child may feel responsible for the marriage breakdown of the parents or for the drinking problem of the mother or father. He or she may have physiological or psychological problems and may be anxious and withdrawn; enuresis and behavioural problems are not uncommon. The child may also have been subject to, or have witnessed, acts of violence or abuse.

The professional should try to make the child feel valued, and that what he or she has to say is important, is helping and is understood. The child should be reassured that he or she is in no way to blame for the parent's problem: it is essential that the child feels safe during disclosures. Appropriate support and interventions will need to be arranged with emphasis on developing the skill required of the child to rebuild social contacts, and find an appropriate place within the family and society.

Other family members

With the permission of the problem drinker and spouse, and having full regard for the rights of an individual to confidentiality, it is often useful to gain additional information from other significant family members during assessment. In most cases the wider family will be aware of the drinking problem and may have offered, or been a good source of, support to the non-drinking spouse or child(ren).

Conclusion

With the correct level of support and advice, and a thorough, properly conducted assessment, the home detoxification experience, and any subsequent interventions, should be beneficial to all those involved.

Additional assistance may be required to deal with accommodation and/or financial difficulties. Referral to appropriate agencies should be made as soon as possible. Special care and attention may be needed to cope with the fears and anxieties engendered by involvement of the social services. The involvement of other agencies does not necessarily have to await the outcome of home detoxification. However, one must protect confidentiality at all times, and ensure that the appropriate permission has been gained.

The family will have to learn how to reward the non-drinking behaviour of the problem drinker in an appropriate way. 'Giving in' to the problem drinker can often be the easiest option available to the already stressed family. How they can deal with this, and what they should do in the eventuality of relapse, should be fully explored prior to detoxification, and advice and support should continue throughout[8].

References

1. Ersser S (1992) A search for the therapeutic dimensions of nurse-patient interaction. In: McMahon R and Pearson A (eds) *Nursing as therapy*. Chapman and Hall, London.

2. Wilson-Barnett J (1984) *Key functions in nursing*. The 1984 Winifred Raphael memorial lecture. Royal College of Nursing, London.

3. Harrè R and Secord PF (1972) *The explanation of social behaviour*. Basil Blackwell, Oxford.

4. Moos, R, Finney J and Chan D (1981) The process of recovery from alcoholism. 1: comparing alcoholic patients and matched community controls. *Journal of Studies on Alcohol*, **42**, 383–402.

5. Oreme T and Rimmer J (1981) Alcoholism and child abuse: a review. *Journal of Studies on Alcohol*, **42**, 273–87.

6. Orford J (1977) Impact of alcoholism on family and home. In: Edwards G and Grant M (eds) *Alcoholism: new knowledge and new responses*. Croom Helm, London.

7. Edwards G (1987) *The treatment of drinking problems: a guide for the helping professions*. Blackwell Scientific Publications, Oxford.

8. Anderson P (1987) Early intervention in general practice. In: Stockwell T and Clement S (eds) *Helping the problem drinker: new initiatives in community care*. Croom Helm, London.

12 Assessment of problem drinkers and drinking problems

The assessment process outlined[1] below to determine suitability can also be part of a pre- and post-detoxification exercise. However, it neither necessarily follows detoxification, nor necessarily requires it.

There are no short cuts to assessments. These must be in depth, including a full assessment of the client's drinking behaviour, antecedents, and the consequences of excessive consumption. A detailed client and family physiological, psychological and social history is also helpful. The following is a guideline to what an assessment should include; although bearing in mind that one must be aware of individual influencing factors, what follows cannot be definitive[1].

A specific assessment procedure for the family has not been included. However, the assessment process outlined herein can adequately be adapted for assessment of the spouse and other family.

Drinking profile

The drinking profile should include:

- usual frequency and quantity of alcohol consumption
- details of the last drinking occasion
- time of day the last alcohol consumption commenced
- whether alcohol is the first drink of the day
- where alcohol consumption takes place
- drinking preferences (eg alone or in company)
- where it is most difficult to control alcohol consumption
- attempts at previous control of drinking or abstinence.

Clients' opinions

Clients' views of their own drinking behaviour and its consequences are important, and indicate the future directions they may wish to follow. Assessment should include asking the client:

- Do you think you have a drink problem?
- Are you an 'alcoholic'?*
- How long have you had a problem with alcohol?
- What do you think is the cause? (eg loneliness, divorce, job loss, bereavement)
- Details of antecedents and consequences.

Family opinions

- How do the family view the drinking problem?
- Is the client a 'problem drinker' or an 'alcoholic'?
- What effects have the drinker's problems had on them?
- Do they agree with the drinker's own assessment of the problem?
- Are they supportive and willing to help?
- What support do they need?
- What help do they feel the drinker needs?

Checklist of complaints

The checklist in Table 12.1 assists in the evaluation of drinking problems, in terms of severity and effects. However, one must stress the importance of eliminating other physical or psychological causative factors, which require additional investigation.

Marital and social effects

Assessment should include problems experienced in the marriage, directly or indirectly associated with the client's drinking problem, as

*Many clients will admit to a drinking problem, but may take offence at the term 'alcoholic', use of which can be detrimental to any future interventions as well as to the client/nurse relationship. Therefore, it is important to identify the individual's level of understanding and acceptance of the problem if a good therapeutic relationship is to be established.

Table 12.1 Checklist of complaints

▪ loss of appetite	▪ gastric upset
▪ ulcers	▪ dyspepsia
▪ morning nausea/vomiting/retching	▪ jaundice
▪ hepatitis	▪ tremor/shakes
▪ depression	▪ anxiety
▪ poor concentration	▪ memory loss or amnesia
▪ epileptic type seizures	▪ sleep disturbances
▪ night sweats	▪ delirium tremens
▪ hallucinations	▪ aggressive behaviour
▪ hyperacusis	▪ tinnitus
▪ itching/crawling sensations	▪ night/morning panics
▪ localized pains/discomfort/muscle cramps	

well as problems in other relationships whether or not they are related to alcohol use and misuse.

Employment

Assessment should include the following:

- Occupation.
- Employed or unemployed.
- Source of income.
- If the client is presently employed:
  - i) What is his or her drinking behaviour at work?
  - ii) Have any warnings been received?
  - iii) How long has the client been employed?
  - iv) Is there a support network attached to the company, such as occupational health?
- Has the client lost any jobs as a direct or indirect result of excessive alcohol consumption?
- How much working time is spent drinking alcohol?
- What is the client's absenteeism record? (alcohol and non-alcohol related)
- Have there been any accidents at work? (what, when and outcome)
- If the client is unemployed, for how long and what is the cause?
- How does the client see his or her future employment needs and direction? Are these realistic?

Housing

Assessment should include:

- type of housing
- whether mortgaged or rented accommodation
- arrears or other problems.

Financial problems

- Are there any financial problems? If YES:
  i) Who are they with?
  ii) What action has been taken to date? (eg to clear, pending court action)
- Is the client or the family in need of advice on money management?
- What advice has already been received, from whom and what was the outcome?

Leisure interests

- Interests prior to and during alcohol misuse.
- What part does the spouse or partner and family play in these?
- How much leisure time is spent drinking?

Influence of others on alcohol consumption

- Include family and friends.
- Do they restrict or increase alcohol consumption, and why?
- Methods used to avoid facing the problems caused by drinking (eg collusion or withdrawal).

Other drugs

- Include current and past medication.
- Prescribed, over-the-counter, and other legal and illegal drug use and misuse.
- Frequency of all drug use, antecedents and consequences.

Hospital admissions and treatments

- Previous treatment (in-patient and out-patient).
- Previous hospital admissions.
- Were these drink related?
  It is useful to be cognizant that hospital admissions or other forms of treatment, which are clearly alcohol or drug related, may not be perceived as such by the client. Information about past alcohol related admissions can be useful when looking in more detail at the consequences of excessive or inappropriate substance misuse and its effects.
- Duration of treatment or hospital admission, and the outcome.

Personality profile

The personality profile should include:

- general characteristics
- likes and dislikes
- interests, rewards and motivations
- topics avoided or found upsetting
- any other information.

History

This area of assessment should include personal and family history, covering both physical and mental health as well as any drinking or drug misuse histories.

Criminal behaviour

This should include:

- convictions past and present
- prison sentences and probation
- activities resulting in conviction (alcohol and non-alcohol related)
- the client's perception of the effects of substance misuse on illegal activities.

Agencies involved with the client and/or family

The tendency is for several statutory and/or voluntary agencies to become involved in the care of clients with alcohol or drug related problems. It is an integral component of the nurse specialist's role to collate and co-ordinate such involvements, and to ensure full and effective communication.

All assessments should include:

- listing of agencies involved
- the reason for involvement
- the present state of involvement and relationship with client.

Agencies include:

- the primary worker
- a community psychiatric nurse
- a community nurse
- a psychiatrist
- the GP
- a health visitor
- a probation officer
- the practice nurse
- Alcoholics Anonymous (AA)
- an alcohol advisory centre
- the county council (eg the housing department)
- a social worker
- voluntary services
- a midwife.

The client's drinking outcome and future drinking plans

A clear picture of the client's future drinking plans and drug use should be clarified as follows:

- Does the client wish to cease drinking altogether, for a short time or not at all?
- Does the client wish to participate in a 'controlled' drinking programme? (Controlled drinking is a structured programme and should not be undertaken by an inexperienced individual without adequate training and supervision.)

- Does the client intend to return to 'social' drinking, or to continue as at present, either with or without further involvement of specialist services?
- Does the client want to reduce alcohol intake?

In addition to establishing the client's view of his or her future, it is important to remember to ask about individuals or agencies who may have helped in the past.

Physical examination

A record should be kept of the client's blood pressure and breathalyzer reading. Arrangements should also be made for appropriate blood tests: blood alcohol concentration (BAC), full blood count (FBC) and liver function test (LFT). Give special attention to the results of the following: gamma glutamyl transferase (Gamma GT); mean corpuscular volume (MCV); alanine aminotransferase (ALT); aspartate aminotransferase (AST); bilirubin.[†]

Care plan

Following a full and systematic assessment, it is essential that a care plan is formulated, and agreed, with the client and all other participants.

References

1. Cooper DB (1985) *The effects of a community alcohol service, the hidden 'potential drinking problems' and problem drinking.* Report to the district management team, Blackburn, Hyndburn and Ribble Valley Health Authority.

2. Stibler H (1991) Carbohydrate-deficient transferrin in serum: a new marker of potentially harmful alcohol consumption reviewed. *Clinical Chemistry*, **37** (12), 2029–37.

[†]Recent research suggests that CDTech, a blood test used to detect carbohydrate-deficient transferrin, has monitoring and detection properties for high continuous alcohol consumption that are superior to those of gamma GT, AST and MCV[2].

13 The home detoxification procedure

The following procedure, assessment tools and records may be adopted in conjunction with a full, systematic and continuing assessment.

Forms to fill

Home detoxification initial assessment form (IAF) (*see* Appendix 1, page 95)

This form allows for the recording of:

- withdrawal syndrome history
- present circumstances
- blood pressure, pulse, temperature and breathalyzer readings
- symptom severity checklist (SSC) and the client's personal score
- home environment assessment (HEA)
- blood test results
- severity of alcohol dependence questionnaire (SADQ) score
- summary of visit
- agreed medication
- next visit arrangements.

It is important to ensure that this is completed as the assessment, and subsequent arrangements for detoxification, progress. A simple but effective procedural checklist is provided on the front of the form.

Home Detoxification Procedural Flow Chart

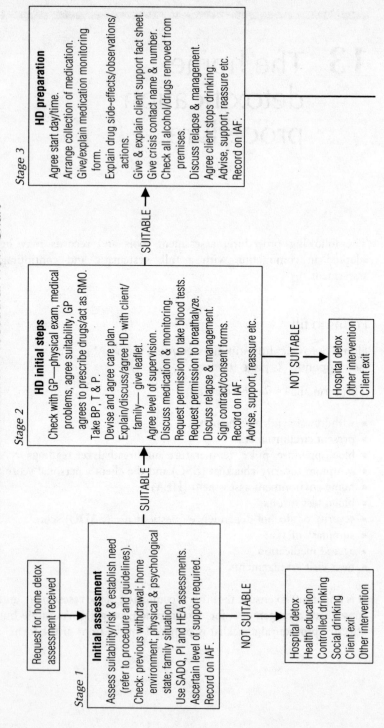

Request for home detox assessment received

Stage 1

Initial assessment

Assess suitability/risk & establish need (refer to procedure and guidelines).
Check: previous withdrawal; home environment; physical & psychological state; family situation.
Use SADQ, PI and HEA assessments.
Ascertain level of support required.
Record on IAF.

NOT SUITABLE

Hospital detox
Health education
Controlled drinking
Social drinking
Client exit
Other intervention

SUITABLE

Stage 2

HD initial steps

Check with GP—physical exam, medical problems, agree suitability, GP agrees to prescribe drugs/act as RMO.
Take BP, T & P.
Devise and agree care plan.
Explain/discuss/agree HD with client/family— give leaflet.
Agree level of supervision.
Discuss medication & monitoring.
Request permission to take blood tests.
Request permission to breathalyze.
Discuss relapse & management.
Sign contract/consent forms.
Record on IAF.
Advise, support, reassure etc.

NOT SUITABLE

Hospital detox
Other intervention
Client exit

SUITABLE

Stage 3

HD preparation

Agree start day/time.
Arrange collection of medication.
Give/explain medication monitoring form.
Explain drug side-effects/observations/ actions.
Give & explain client support fact sheet.
Give crisis contact name & number.
Check all alcohol/drugs removed from premises.
Discuss relapse & management.
Agree client stops drinking.
Advise, support, reassure etc.
Record on IAF.

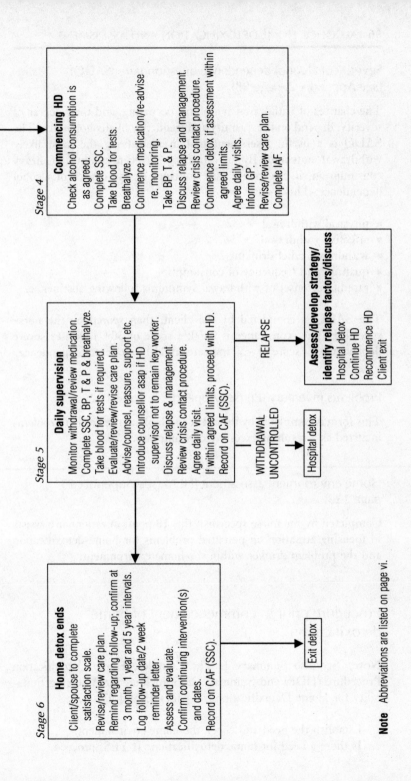

Stage 4

Commencing HD

Check alcohol consumption is as agreed.
Complete SSC.
Take blood for tests.
Breathalyze.
Commence medication/re-advise re. monitoring.
Take BP, T & P.
Discuss relapse and management.
Review crisis contact procedure.
Commence detox if assessment within agreed limits.
Agree daily visits.
Inform GP.
Revise/review care plan.
Complete IAF.

Stage 5

Daily supervision

Monitor withdrawal/review medication.
Complete SSC, BP, T & P & breathalyze.
Take blood for tests if required.
Evaluate/review/revise care plan.
Advise/counsel, reassure, support etc.
Introduce counsellor asap if HD supervisor not to remain key worker.
Discuss relapse & management.
Review crisis contact procedure.
Agree daily visit.
If within agreed limits, proceed with HD.
Record on CAF (SSC).

RELAPSE →

WITHDRAWAL UNCONTROLLED →

Hospital detox

Assess/develop strategy/ identify relapse factors/discuss

Hospital detox
Continue HD
Recommence HD
Client exit

Stage 6

Home detox ends

Client/spouse to complete satisfaction scale.
Revise/review care plan.
Remind regarding follow-up; confirm at 3 month, 1 year and 5 year intervals.
Log follow-up date/2 week reminder letter.
Assess and evaluate.
Confirm continuing intervention(s) and dates.
Record on CAF (SSC).

Exit detox →

Note Abbreviations are listed on page vi.

Severity of alcohol dependence questionnaire (SADQ)
(*see* Appendix 2, page 98)

The chances of withdrawal symptoms occurring, and their degree of severity, depend on the quantity and frequency of alcohol intake. The SADQ is a useful assessment tool in identifying the most likely withdrawal outcome. By investigating a recent month of heavy consumption, it can give a pure measure of the degree of alcohol dependence. This focuses on:

- physical withdrawal
- affective withdrawal
- withdrawal relief drinking
- quantity and frequency of consumption
- rapidity of onset of withdrawal symptoms following abstinence.

The SADQ is completed by the client, then scored by the nurse specialist. The score range is 0–60; a score of 30+ indicates severe dependency; a score of –30 indicates mild to moderate dependence.

Problems inventory (PI) *(see* Appendix 3, page 102)

This form is completed by the client and looks at the level of problems incurred as a result of excessive consumption.

Home environment assessment (HEA) (*see* Appendix 13, page 123)

Completed by the nurse specialist, this 10 point questionnaire assists in focusing attention on potential problems for home detoxification and the problem drinker within the home environment.

Procedure prior to commencement of home detoxification

Note See also Summary 1: The Complete Home Detoxification Procedure (HDP) and Summary 2: Guidelines for Assessing Suitability for Home Detoxification (on pages 85 and 92).

1   Establish the need and check the home environment.
2   Is there a need for home detoxification? If YES, proceed.

3 Describe the detoxification procedure to the client and the family. Give them a leaflet (Appendix 4, page 104).
4 Check with the GP: does he or she envisage any problems with home detoxification and is he or she prepared to act as the responsible medical officer (RMO)?
5 Arrange for the client to see the GP if necessary.
6 Request permission to take blood for liver function test (LFT), full blood count (FBC) and blood alcohol concentration (BAC).
7 Discuss the medication regime and agree boundaries with the GP, client and family.
8 Arrange prescription collection.
9 Give the medication monitoring booklet to a relative or friend (Appendix 5, page 108).
10 Sign contracts with the client (Appendix 6, page 109) and family (Appendix 7, page 111)
11 Complete the IAF checklist.
12 Establish future plans and the programme.
13 Agree on a commencement date for home detoxification, and commence.
14 Discuss management in the event of relapse, and crisis action.
15 Give the client a contact number; advise on emergency and crisis contact.

Procedure at the commencement of home detoxification

1 Keep the IAF up to date.
2 Complete the SSC. (Appendices 8 and 9, pages 113 and 115).
Record the score on the IAF. Each question on this checklist of withdrawal symptoms is rated 0–3. A total score of 18+ should indicate concern; in such instances, contact the GP before proceeding.
3 Breathalyze—record results on IAF.
4 Take blood samples (with prior permission).
5 Take blood pressure, temperature and pulse, and record them on the IAF. Refer any problems to the GP, before commencing detoxification.
6 Commence medication.
7 Reaffirm emergency contact points.
8 Review future plans and the programme.

Daily assessment

Complete the home detoxification continuing assessment form (CAF) (Appendix 10, page 116) daily. This form contains provisions for recording all the following information. It also contains a daily SSC.

1 Monitor medication at each visit (*see* Chapter 14). Look for signs of 'over sedation' (eg drowsiness, rapid fall in blood pressure) and 'under sedation' (eg increase in withdrawal symptoms, nausea, headache, sweating, itching). Review as necessary and within agreed boundaries.
2 Complete the daily SSC, which is part of the CAF.
3 Breathalyze client and record the result on the CAF.
4 Take and record blood pressure, temperature and pulse daily.
5 Advise, counsel, support and reassure as needed.
6 Review future plans and the programme.
7 If all results are within the agreed limits, proceed with detoxification.

Arrangements should be made as soon as possible to introduce the primary worker or counsellor to the client and the family. This is particularly important if the nurse specialist undertaking the detoxification is not continuing in a support role after this process has been completed.

At the end of home detoxification

Ask the client and the family to complete the satisfaction scale (Appendices 11 and 12, pages 119 and 121) and review any future interventions and programmes. Go through the early warning signs and dangers of relapse with them, and reaffirm methods of emergency contact. Arrange future follow-up dates and times.

14 Detoxification medication

The drugs used during home detoxification are often the preferred choice of the GP, agreed upon after full discussion with the nurse specialist. However, it is important to ensure that any prescription given to assist the client through alcohol withdrawal is limited and specific—that is, given over an agreed duration and reducing in dosage throughout the agreed time, as symptoms desist. It is also important, especially in view of the computerization of many general practices, to remove the prescription from the presenting list once detoxification is over.

The client should be advised of the dangers of driving or operating machinery while taking drugs which assist during detoxification.

Before detoxification commences one must agree on boundaries and manoeuvrability, for adjustment of medication, with the GP. Any adjustment above or below the agreed amount must be renegotiated.

Chlordiazepoxide

The drug now most commonly preferred to alleviate withdrawal symptoms is chlordiazepoxide (Librium). This is usually administered orally, 25–100 mg, three or four times per day. The dose is reduced over a 5–9 day period.

Whatever the prescribed medication, the nurse needs to be alerted to the dangers of possible over- or under-sedation during home detoxification. Chlordiazepoxide may cause drowsiness, dizziness, ataxia, dry mouth, headache and occasionally confusion. The effects of this drug are increased with alcohol. It is important to avoid prolonged use and abrupt withdrawal. On the other hand, under-sedation will result in complaints of increased intensity of withdrawal symptoms.

Chlormethiazole

Chlormethiazole (Heminevrin) has until recently been the drug of choice during alcohol withdrawal. However, because of the potentially lethal outcome if combined with alcohol[1], association with possible liver damage, and the danger of dependency on the drug itself, chlormethiazole is fast losing favour.

The Committee on Safety of Medicine[1] has issued clear instructions relating to the use of chlormethiazole in alcohol withdrawal. These state: 'When used in the control of symptoms arising from acute withdrawal from alcohol, close hospital supervision is required.' The Committee went on to state that chlormethiazole must only be used 'in exceptional circumstances, by out-patients in specialist units'. In view of these potential hazards, the author would advise against the use of this drug for home detoxification.

Evening primrose oil

A great deal of research has been undertaken into the effects of evening primrose oil (trade names include Efamol, Epogam and Efamast)[2-6], which is rich in gamma-linolenic acid, as an alternative to the above medications. The primary advantage of evening primrose oil must be the lack of potential dependency problems and complications of overdose. Its use in alcohol withdrawal continues to be discussed and should not be dismissed lightly, although the advantages in home detoxification have yet to be fully explored. The door is perhaps open to further research.

Carbamazepine

There is an increasing trend towards the use of carbamazepine which, it has been suggested, has fewer side-effects and dependency problems than other currently favoured drugs.

In their double-blind study, using carbamazepine versus Oxazepam in alcohol detoxification, Stuppaeck et al.[7] suggested that carbamazepine was 'at least as effective as Oxazepam' and that is showed 'statistically significant superiority on days six and seven' of treatment.

The trial drug regime follows a nine day reducing dose as outlined below:

Days 1–3—carbamazepine 800 mg (200 mg → 200 mg → 400 mg)
Days 4–7—carbamazepine 600 mg (divided into three doses)
Day 8—carbamazepine 200 mg (bid)
Day 9—carbamazepine 200 mg (nocte)

The results look promising, and there is clearly a need for more research into this drug. It might be suitable as the research component of a new detoxification project.

Vitamin replacement

Prophylactic oral drug therapy to replace vitamin deficiency is essential for all clients undertaking home detoxification. Vitamins B_1 (thiamine), B_6 (pyridoxine) and C (ascorbic acid), are important nutrients normally deficient in the problem drinker who has been consuming excessive amounts of alcohol. It has been suggested that as many as 60%[8,9] of problem drinkers are likely to be vitamin deficient and will require high potency vitamin therapy to maintain adequate levels of the water soluble B and C vitamins[10,11]. Therefore, replacement is essential as a preventive measure against the onset of Wernicke's encephalopathy (*see* pages 8–9).

Vitamin preparations such as Orovite (tablet or granules), Becosym (tablet or syrup), or oral thiamine hydrochloride, will be adequate in most cases.

Parentrovite

The practice of administering intramuscular (im) Parentrovite is still used by some nurse specialists, and in cases of severe vitamin deficiency is the most effective way of ensuring essential vitamin replacement. However, this form of vitamin therapy is presently losing favour in home detoxification because of the possibility of anaphylaxis and the questionability of administering such painful injections when oral medication will produce the same effect in the majority of cases.

However, as Parentrovite is still the vitamin replacement drug of choice for some practitioners, it is appropriate that advice and attention should be given to its use.

It is essential that one carefully assesses the needs of each individual, and acts accordingly in the client's interest. If Parentrovite is to be administered im during home detoxification, then the nurse specialist must be aware of the potential problem of anaphylactic shock and how first aid should be administered (*see* pages 63–4). Whilst anaphylactic shock is rare, it should be made clear that this reactive state can kill if appropriate intervention is not administered quickly and effectively.

Parentrovite 1+2, high potency im, is usually administered over a period of seven days. It is a rather large and painful injection; the following 'tips' may be of help in reducing the trauma.

- Administering Parentrovite when it is cold increases the pain. Warm the ampoule in the hand prior to drawing up.
- Intramuscular Parentrovite should always be administered in the upper outer quadrant of the buttock. Alternating the buttock (ie left side on day one, right side on day two) will reduce the amount of trauma to one site.
- It may be appropriate to administer Parentrovite im every other day, rather than daily.

Finally, always question if it is really an essential alternative to oral vitamin replacement.

Breathalyzer use

An understanding must be achieved with the client that any medication is issued only if he or she agrees to comply with daily breathalyzer tests as agreed in the detoxification contract, and that these readings must be within the agreed limit.

Anaphylactic shock

Anaphylactic shock following Parentrovite injection is a rare occurrence. However, it is essential that the nurse specialist supervising home detoxification is appropriately trained in the first aid response to this condition, and how one should implement appropriate

Table 14.1   Reactions to parenteral injection

- tightness in the chest
- sneezing
- coughing
- urticaria
- dyspnoea
- cyanosis
- tissue swelling (eyelids, lips, tongue, hands and feet)
- laryngeal oedema
- bronchospasm resulting in respiratory distress and insufficiency

home-based treatment to maintain the client's well being until appropriate medical intervention is available. What follows is a basic theoretical guide and must not replace appropriately supervised tuition.

Anaphylactic shock is a severe reaction which usually occurs after a second injection of a foreign protein has been administered. If it is not treated effectively, it can prove fatal.

A reaction follows very rapidly after parenteral injection and the client may experience several of the symptoms outlined in Table 14.1.

The blood pressure decreases and the pulse is rapid and weak. The client's skin is pale and feels cold, the pupils are dilated, and the client may lose consciousness. These are warning signs of cardiorespiratory failure or severe shock.

Urgent attention is needed to prevent a fatal reaction. The nurse specialist should carry an emergency anaphylactic shock pack and be fully cognizant of its use.

The primary nursing responsibility is to maintain life until appropriate medical intervention arrives. The aims are to:

- maintain ventilation
- support the cardiovascular system
- decrease the hypersensitivity response
- alleviate psychological distress
- prevent future reactions.

Specific nursing first aid required in anaphylactic shock

Maintenance of airways and oxygen intake

1 Place the client in recumbent position with the neck extended.
2 If the client loses consciousness, and the tongue is blocking the passage of air, introduce an airway.

3 Use suction to remove bronchial secretion.
4 Oxygen should be administered as soon as it is available to decrease hypoxia (lack of oxygen in the tissues) resulting from respiratory insufficiency.
5 Cardiopulmonary resuscitation (CPR) may be necessary if the client collapses.

Circulatory support
1 Remove tight clothing.
2 Elevate the lower body.
3 Monitor vital signs at 10–15 minute intervals.
4 As soon as possible, an intravenous infusion should be established to increase intravascular volume.

Decreasing the hypersensitivity reaction
The administration of medication and doses will depend on local policy and procedure, and appropriate medical prescription, which the nurse specialist should be familiar with. An indication of drug use and route is given below.

Psychological support
Anaphylactic shock is a very frightening experience and the seriousness of the situation is quickly sensed by the client. Quiet, quick and confident reassurance is essential.

Drug administration in anaphylactic shock

A 1 : 000 adrenalin solution (1 mg/ml), 0.5–1 ml for adults, may be prescribed and administered by injection. This is generally given in small repeated doses to relax bronchial and laryngeal spasms if respiratory distress persists.

A corticosteroid preparation, such as hydrocortisone or prednisolone, is administered to reduce tissue sensitivity.

Special care should be taken in cases of hyperthyroidism, diabetes mellitus, ischaemic heart disease, hypertension and elderly patients. Side-effects include anxiety, tremor, tachycardia, arrhythmias, dry mouth and cold extremities[12].

References

1. Committee on Safety of Medicine (1987) Fatal interactions between Heminevrin and alcohol. *Current Problems*, no. 20.

2. Corbett R, Berthou F, Leonard BE *et al.* (1992) Rapid communication. The effects of chronic administration of ethanol on synaptosomal fatty acid composition: modulation by oil enriched with gamma-linolenic acid. *Alcohol and Alcoholism*, **27** (1), 11–14.

3. Horrobin DF (1984) Prostaglandins (PGs) and essential fatty acids (EFAs): a new approach to the understanding and treatment of alcoholism. *Psychiatry in Practice*, August issue, 19–21.

4. Horrobin DF and Mehar MS (1980) Possible role of prostaglandin E_1 in the affective disorders and in alcoholism. *British Medical Journal*, **280**, 1363–6.

5. Rotrosen J, Mandio D, Segarnick D *et al.* (1980). Ethanol and prostaglandin E_1: biochemical and behavioural interactions. *Life Sciences*, **26**, 1867–76.

6. Varma PK and Persaud TVN (1982) Protection against ethanol-induced embryonic damage by administering gamma-linolenic acids. *Prostaglandins Leukotrienes and Medicine*, **8**, 641–5.

7. Stuppaeck CH, Pycha R, Miller C *et al.* (1992). Carbamazepine versus Oxazepam in the treatment of alcohol withdrawal: a double-blind study. *Alcohol and Alcoholism*, **27** (2), 153–8.

8. Majumdar SK, Shaw GK and Thomson AD (1981) Blood vitamin status in chronic alcoholics after a single dose of polyvitamin: a preliminary report. *Postgraduate Medical Journal*, **57**, 164–6.

9. Shaw GK and Thompson AD (1977) A joint psychiatric and medical out-patient clinic for alcoholics. In: Edwards G and Grant M (eds) *Alcoholism: new knowledge and new responses*, pp 328–34. Croom Helm, London.

10. Leading article (1979) *British Medical Journal*, **2** (6185), 291–2.

11. Editorial (1979) Wernicke's preventable encephalopathy. *The Lancet*, **I**, 1122–3.

12. British National Formulary (1992) 23rd issue. British Medical Association and Royal Pharmaceutical Society.

15 Relapse

What follows is not exhaustive. However, it does highlight some of the contributing factors that may lead to relapse. Why one problem drinker relapses during or after detoxification and another does not, is attributable to a broad range of factors, only some of which are known. The conditioning of past treatments and doctoring by such bodies as Alcoholics Anonymous (AA), in the disease model approach to the problem, may be one contributing factor (although it would be wrong to knock the help they have offered to many individuals, and AA is still a reasonable option for some clients). The concept of 'one drink—one drunk' may lead the individual with a drink problem to believe that he or she has 'failed', and may consequently encourage continuation towards 'rock bottom'. This idea that one has yet to reach rock bottom can, and does, promote inappropriate drinking behaviour in some problem drinkers.

Heather and Robertson[1] suggest that what is often interpreted by others as relapse may in fact be the problem drinker's attempt to return to 'normal' social drinking.

Relapse, as well as being a problem for the client, often involves mixed emotions and disappointment for the nurse and the family. Therefore, it is important to be aware of this; as well as providing the appropriate intervention for the client and the family, one should also seek an active support network for oneself.

When relapse occurs, there is an urgent need to examine the causative factors. From the moment client contact commences, the concept of 'one drink—one drunk' should be discussed, and preferably discharged. It is a myth that, if one makes even a minor slip on the road to sensible drinking or total abstinence (whatever the chosen goal), all will then be lost and the continuance of self-destruction becomes inevitable. One should encourage the client to come forward and actively examine the real reasons for the relapse, rather than continuing to hide behind the substance of misuse.

Relapse is a common event amongst substance misusers and lasting success often involves much trial and error. In some cases, relapse can be viewed as an attempt by the problem drinker to return to 'normal' levels of alcohol consumption. This needs to be understood, and one should not regard the client as 'falling from grace'. However, any relapse must be taken seriously by the client, family, nurse and all other professionals involved.

If the relationship between the client and the primary worker is one of trust, this will facilitate openness when discussing the precipitating factors of relapse. The client and the family must feel able to seek out the nurse for help, rather than avoiding any contact because of guilt, shame, and feelings of failure and inadequacy, which are often associated with relapse.

Relapse can be planned and explosive, unplanned and explosive, or observed as a gradual slide back to excessive consumption over an extended period of time. The duration of relapse depends on many factors and influences. It may be short-lived, lasting no more than a few days, or it can last for a few months or even years.

A comprehensive model of change

Prochaska and DiClemente[2] suggest that relapse forms part of a change process cycle (Figure 15.1). The individual may leave the cycle at relapse, or exit after achieving a permanent change in behaviour. Their model suggests that relapse in itself is not an end, and that the individual can re-enter the change process at any future stage. In their paper, it was suggested that 'relapsers were found to respond like a combination of contemplators and people in action'.

The 'integrative model of change'[3] puts forward this theory and one would suggest that all nurse specialists in the substance misuse field should be familiar with the model. At the end of this guide, a further reading list has been added and it is hoped that the reader will develop his or her knowledge in this area (*see* page 126).

Many individuals with alcohol or drug dependency problems change their addictive behaviour following a direct change in life events; for example, a change in relationship, redundancy, employment, accident or illness, birth of a child, or the death of a close family member. These life events may curtail, neutralize, or in some cases enhance, the carer's endeavours with the client[4]. All professionals involved in the care of the individual with a dependency problem must take account of these changes, when formulating treatment programmes and planning interventions, if their involvement is to be of therapeutic benefit.

An holistic and eclectic approach is essential, and the nurse should be prepared to intervene with a comprehensive set of change activities when appropriate[4].

It has been suggested that there are as many as 250 different therapies available to the individual with a dependency problem[5]. In 1984, a multi-professional conference was held with the aim to 'develop a more comprehensive model of change for the treatment of addictive behaviours'[3]. Agreement was reached that any model developed must apply to the whole range of individuals, from those requiring maximum intervention (in-patient care) to those needing minimal intervention (self-help manuals)[3].

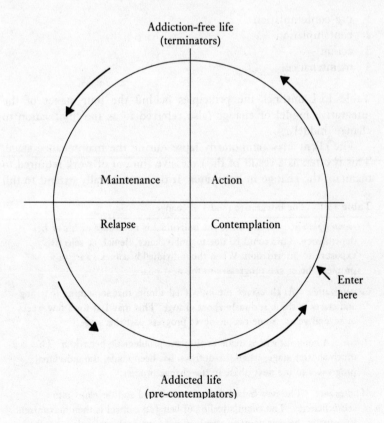

Figure 15.1   An integrative model of change cycle

Prochaska and DiClemente's model is applicable to a variety of dependency behaviours and, at the same time, advances one's understanding of how people change, for example from initial awareness of a problem to the stage where the problem no longer exists.

This framework assists professionals in the organization of their knowledge, and improves decision-making processes in client management. The model takes account of the client who self-changes, as well as the individual progressing through therapy. It helps the nurse therapist to integrate the various treatment methods immediately available, and encompasses the change process from problem recognition to resolution.

Prochaska and DiClemente[3] describe their model of change as three dimensional, in that it integrates changes, processes and levels of change, and comprises four stages:

1 pre-contemplation
2 contemplation
3 action
4 maintenance.

Table 15.1 outlines the principles behind the four stages of the integrative model of change (also referred to as the 'motivation to change' model).

The client may temporarily lapse during the maintenance stage. This is often as a result of the excessive amount of work required to maintain the change in behaviour. It does not usually extend to full

Table 15.1 The integrative model of change

Pre-contemplation. At this stage the individual is not aware of his or her dependency. This could be due to ambivalence, denial, or selective exposure to information. When the individual becomes aware of a problem, he or she progresses to the next phase.

Contemplation. At this stage the individual admits that something is wrong and starts to think seriously about change. This may last for a few weeks or several years. Some people never progress past this stage.

Action. A commitment is made to alter the problematic behaviour. This is a much shorter stage; when the decision has been made, the individual progresses to the next phase in the change process.

Maintenance. The new behaviour is strengthened and develops into self-efficiency. The client's feeling of being in control is then maximized. Eventually the exit point to termination of the problem cycle is reached.

relapse. However, clients who do experience complete relapse may go back to the pre-contemplation stage and rejoin the cycle at a later date.

Research into relapse amongst people with dependency behaviours has indicated that 70–80% of those attempting to modify their behaviour relapse within the first year[6,7]. However, 84% of those who relapse subsequently return to the pre-contemplation stage[3]. Most self-changers, it has been suggested, make at least three serious revolutions of the change cycle before exiting into a relatively dependency free life[8,9]. Nevertheless, some individuals do become entrenched in one particular stage of change[4].

If the nurse–client relationship is to be therapeutic, it is essential that they work through the same stages of the change process. Resistance to therapeutic interventions often comes as a direct result of the client and nurse working at differing stages. Prochaska and DiClemente[3] clearly indicate the importance of mutual understanding:

'The more directive, action orientated therapist would find a client who is at the contemplation stage highly resistive to therapy. From the client's perspective, however, the therapist may be seen to be wanting to move too quickly . . . A therapist who specializes in contemplating and understanding the causes of problems will tend to see the client who is ready for action as resistive to the insight aspect of therapy. The client would be warned against acting impulsively. From the client's perspective . . . the therapist might be warned against moving too slowly'.

Nurses are therefore warned that, like their clients, they too can easily become entrenched in a favourite stage of change.

Factors which may lead to relapse

If relapse occurs early in the treatment process, it could indicate that motivation is still lacking.

It is possible that the client may not have sufficient coping skills required to defend the chosen goal. There is an understanding of what is wanted, but the client cannot live up to the intention.

Some problem drinkers may find their abstinence or reduced intake unrewarding. This type of relapse usually occurs after 6–12 months of uneasy abstinence or controlled drinking. In such cases, additional work is required on alternative, more rewarding, strategies. These may include the benefits of improved finances or health, as well as alternative recreational activities such as revival of old hobbies or skills.

The client may be unable to cope with mood disturbances as a result of reduced consumption or abstinence. Experience of patches of gloom, irritability, anxiety, craving and depression may overwhelm the defences. If there is, or has been, an underlying mental health problem not previously diagnosed, the client may find it increasingly difficult to cope with this. For example, alcohol may have been used to control anxiety or panic attacks, and when this is removed the precipitating problems are exacerbated and lead to the seeking of relief.

Minor life events, which can seem trivial to outsiders, may 'build up' and become a causative factor in relapse—eg an angry exchange with the spouse or partner, problems with the car or an unexpectedly large repair bill.

The failure of the client to be vigilant when entering known problem areas and situations is also a potential hazard which requires full exploration. Immediate rewards, such as the effect of a glass of wine as a social lubricant at a friend's party, can outweigh the long-term consequences of excessive alcohol use. As memories of past dependency fade, it is easy to believe that one can once more 'get away with it'.

The client and the family must be alerted to a potential relapse and they should prepare appropriate emergency strategies with the nurse to deal with such situations. However, the nurse, client and family need to be aware that relapses are not terminal, nor are they inevitable.

References

1. Heather N and Robertson I (1983) *Controlled drinking*. Methuen, London.

2. Prochaska JO and DiClemente CC (1983) Stages and process of self-change of smoking: towards an integrative model of change. *Journal of Consulting and Clinical Psychology*, **51** (3), 390–5.

3. Prochaska JO and DiClemente CC (1986) Towards a comprehensive model of change. In: Miller WR and Heather N (eds) *Treating addictive behaviours—process of change*. Plenum, London.

4. Davidson R (1991) Facilitating change in problem drinkers. In: Davidson R, Rollnick S and MacEwan I (eds) *Counselling problem drinkers*. Routledge, London.

5. Parloff M (1980) Psychotherapy and research: an anaclitic depression. *Psychiatry*, **43**, 279–93.

6. Hunt W, Barnett L and Branch L (1971) Relapse rate in addiction programmes. *Journal of Clinical Psychology*, **27**, 455–6.

7. Olcott P (1985) Perceived change processes in successful weight loss. Unpublished doctoral dissertation, University of Rhodes Island.

8. Prochaska JO and DiClemente CC (1983) Self-change processes, self-efficiency and decisional balance across five stages of smoking cessation. In: Engstram P (ed) *Advances in cancer control*. AR Liss, New York.

9. Schacter S (1982) Recidivism and self-care of smoking and obesity. *American Psychologist*, **37**, 436–44.

16 The importance of research

Nursing is a research based profession. Drug and alcohol nurses must maintain detailed and accurate accounts of their activities, and the effect these have on the client, family, fellow professionals and voluntary services. It is not enough to say that what they do, or that the services they offer, is appropriate to the needs of the individual. The science of nursing cannot progress without substantiated data which highlight the effects of one's activities.

Nurses involved in active research into home detoxification, and other service provisions offered by voluntary and statutory substance misuse agencies, are in a prime position to evaluate the effectiveness of therapeutic interventions. They can also influence their development and the appropriate service response.

An NHS general manager is not in a position to accept that a given method or approach is good or bad, unless this has been substantiated. Often decisions to close down a service are made solely on the basis that it would save money. Alcohol and drug services are often unnecessarily under threat, yet adequate data is available within the service which, if properly evaluated, would substantiate the arguments of service effectiveness and development.

On the other hand, a service which chooses not to make itself available to clients because it has not enough staff cannot argue for an increase in staffing ratio to meet additional demands: there is insufficient proof that these exist.

One often hears about wild and unsubstantiated claims. What follows was reported to have been discussed in depth at a recent meeting of professionals, about home detoxification. It was suggested that, if a client undergoing home detoxification holds his or her own medication, which is supervised by the nurse specialist, then the client rather than the nurse should accept responsibility for any complications arising from severe withdrawal symptoms.

Such an assumption has frightening ramifications. The client cannot be responsible for regulating his or her medication; the problem drinker's responsibility is to take the medication 'as prescribed'. The idea that clients are responsible for their subsequent welfare is *not* based on sound nursing practice and has *no* scientific backing. It is simply an excuse to 'opt out' of one's responsibility.

It is the nurse supervisor's responsibility to ensure that the detoxification is progressing 'within normal limits', and that steps are taken to monitor withdrawal and subsequent interventions initiated if the symptoms increase or decrease. Nurses need to remember that, as professionals, they are responsible and accountable for their actions *and* omissions[1,2].

Research must be an integral part of any substance misuse project and should form part of the operational policy and individual job descriptions. Appropriate training relating to research methods should be given to all staff.

Nurse specialists should also take steps to ensure that they remain aware of all new research developments, and should critically appraise these. Failure to do so will result in outdated practices, which could be detrimental to the outcome of client intervention.

Finally, research knowledge is for sharing. If it is to be of benefit to anyone, it cannot be a secret. Research exists in order that its findings can improve practices and interventions for all, and especially those we care for.

Reference

1. United Kingdom Central Council for Nursing, Midwifery and Health Visiting (1992) *Code of professional conduct*. Third edition. UKCC, London.

2. United Kingdom Central Council for Nursing, Midwifery and Health Visiting (1992) *Standards for the administration of medicines*. UKCC, London.

17 The new service provision: PR and getting started

Communication

Communication is the key to success in community service development, and it is an essential component of the drug and alcohol specialties. The key tasks listed in Table 17.1 cannot be stressed enough.

One should *never* assume that service purchasers, providers and/or users (other professionals, voluntary agencies, clients, family and significant others) know what the service offers them. Even if you have explained over and over again. The service may be a significant part of your professional life, but often it is only a small part of the activity undertaken by the person or organization you are dealing with.

Communicating with the media

Always try to appoint in advance one easily available public relations person. This person should have specialist knowledge in the drug and alcohol field so that he or she can give clear and specific advice and answers to any questions raised. This individual will tell the press, radio and TV what it is you are doing, what you do not do, and how to access your service.

Table 17.1   Key tasks in service communication and networking

1   Make contact (through all media, especially personal contact).
2   Maintain contact.
3   Keep doing it (repeat contact).
4   Reinforce (always state and restate who you are, what it is you do, and what you do not do).

Always be brief, clear and to the point when talking to the press. Anyone who has had dealings with them will know that what has been said can sometimes be misrepresented. This is an occupational hazard which will happen at some stage; expect it and prepare well.

Many district health authorities will allow only a senior manager to communicate with the media, but this person is probably not the one best qualified for the job. All too often, managers' lack of knowledge shows very quickly. Therefore, let the better informed do it, and then the message will get across.

Supplying information

Circulate information on home detoxification before the service starts. Include a start date, a contact person, what is offered, what is not offered, referral forms, who can refer, service times and what to do in an emergency.

This information should go to *all* service managers (statutory and voluntary sectors), GPs, community nurses, practice nurses, health visitors, community psychiatric nurses, midwives, home helps, social workers, probation officers, directors of voluntary services (eg the Citizen's Advice Bureau) and the Community Health Council. Always invite contact.

The individuals who are to be the first point of contact, and who will undertake the home detoxification, should make a personal visit to each prospective referral agent, for full verbal explanation of the service. Stress the importance of communication and joint assessment, and on leaving hand out:

- referral forms and method instructions
- contact names and points, and times available
- information leaflets.

Before the launch

Pre-launch arrangements

Before the service launch, prepare well and ensure that all the information is at hand and pre-launch arrangements have been made. Table 17.2 lists some of the paperwork, handouts, contracts, agreements, policies and procedures required prior to the launch date.

Table 17.2   Pre-launch documentation, contracts and agreements

- information sheets
- leaflets
- standard letters
- procedures and policies
- press releases
- referral forms
- assessment tools
- research paperwork/computer programming
- equipment and service facilities
- blood test processing
- ethics committee approval

Going public

The best way of letting the public know about a new service is to tell them about it. Issue a press release two weeks prior to commencement of the service to the local press, radio and TV. Briefly introduce the subject: 'coming soon—watch this space'.

Try and obtain interviews to explain the aims and function of the service. Be clear, be brief and state what you do and do not do, and who can refer. In addition, give information on sensible drinking, things to look out for in excessive alcohol use, and health problems; quote some statistics to indicate the size of the problem, and talk about the benefits to the client and the family, and in terms of costs—ie savings on in-patient costs and the potential benefits to prevention strategies from this leftover money.

Launch day

Organize a launch day and invite VIPs to the operational base to meet the team and examine the facilities. It is important to ensure that a senior representative of the service, who is competent and capable of providing answers to queries, is at the entrance to greet and direct, and generally pander to, the needs of the invited guests. One should always prepare in advance for disasters and have a strategy ready for all eventualities.

Arrange a brief talk on the aims and objectives of the service, highlighting the partnership between you, the agency and the client requesting your intervention. Have plenty of well versed 'volunteers' around who are capable of answering, in detail, any questions arising from the talk.

If possible, invite the local MP, parish, district and county councillors, the mayor and executive officers of statutory and voluntary agencies, especially the general managers, directors of social services, GPs and consultants in mental and general health. Don't forget occupational health officers from the private sector who are possible purchasers, the chair and secretary of the Community Health Council, service managers, and heads of the social services, probation, the Citizen's Advice Bureau (CAB), Age Concern, etc. Put out a press call to cover the event.

A low alcohol (education starts at home) wine and cheese buffet is often a good idea. Give out leaflets and information as described earlier.

Continuing public relations

Try to organize high profile media events at intervals to raise public and professional awareness of the service, availability, and the mode of access. Whenever possible, hand out leaflets and advise on method of contact and availability times.

Ideas for events include:

- low alcohol and alcohol-free wine tastings
- seminars and conferences
- 'drinkwise' days
- fun runs
- parachute jumps.

Remember health promotion *at all times*.

Referrals

Assess all referrals for suitability for home detoxification within 24–48 hours of receipt and feed back to the referring agent (and the GP if he or she is not the referring agent). Be aware of the ethics of client confidentiality (Chapter 18).

18 When referrals arrive

Communication

- Make contact with the referrer—if possible in person, if not, then by telephone. Follow up all contacts in writing and later in person.
- Contact the GP by telephone if he or she is not the referrer.
- Write and telephone (or see personally) both of the above after each assessment. Inform them of what has been agreed and not agreed. Confirm and agree their roles.
- At the end of home detoxification, write and telephone (or make personal contact) with the referrer/GP, and give feedback on outcome.
- Use prepared standard letters, with phrases such as: 'Thank you for your referral'; 'He refused help'; 'We are unable to contact the client'.

    If there is nothing at that stage you can do, explain why and agree on reassessment plans and procedure. Offer an alternative and/or advice on future management.

Confidentiality

Whilst it has been stressed that communication is the key (Chapter 17), it is imperati, e that one maintains the highest standards of confidentiality. Always agree with the client what contact can and cannot be made. Ensure that his or her decision is based on full information, which is fully understood. All nurses are bound by the UK Central Council (UKCC) code of professional conduct and guidelines on accountability, which set out the ethical obligations to the client[1,2], and must be cognizant of the requirements laid down in the UKCC *Scope of professional practice* and *Standards for records and record keeping*[3,4].

The exchange of information is often of paramount importance to the continuing care of the individual requesting your intervention and skills. However, only specific and relevant information should be exchanged so that the client's privacy is respected.

Support

It is important to maintain an effective support network within any organization. For those working within the drug and alcohol specialism, there is an increased need to gain knowledge of new developments, and to seek external support for oneself.

The following organizations can give help.

The Addictions Forum
Alcohol Research Group
University of Edinburgh
Morningside Park
Edinburgh EH10 5HF
Tel: 031 447 2011
Chair: Dr Douglas Cameron
Membership Secretary: Professor Martin Plant

Association of Nurses in Substance Abuse (ANSA)
The Secretary
CDTIC
Theatre Court
London Road
Northwich
CW9 5HB
Tel: 0606 49055

Alcohol Concern
275 Gray's Inn Road
London WC1X 8QF
Tel: 071 833 3471

Medical Council on Alcoholism
1 St Andrew's Place
London NW1 4LB
Tel: 071 487 44445

RCN Substance Misuse Forum
Royal College of Nursing
20 Cavendish Square
London W1M 0AB
Chair: Anthony Sheehan

David B Cooper
'Sunset'
7 Stour Close
Glemsford
Sudbury
Suffolk CO10 7UB

References

1. United Kingdom Central Council for Nursing, Midwifery and Health Visiting (1992) *Code of professional conduct*. Third edition. UKCC, London.

2. United Kingdom Central Council for Nursing, Midwifery and Health Visiting (1989) *Exercising accountability*. UKCC, London.

3. United Kingdom Central Council for Nursing, Midwifery and Health Visiting (1992) *The scope of professional practice*. UKCC, London.

4. United Kingdom Central Council for Nursing, Midwifery and Health Visiting (1992) *Standards for records and record keeping*. UKCC, London.

19 Conclusion

Treatment, and other therapeutic interventions, can commence immediately one makes contact with the client and the family. However, assessment must continue throughout if any such interventions are to be effective and beneficial.

From the information carefully gathered during assessment, planning, implementation and evaluation can take place, not just for the period of detoxification, but beyond that point and even after the nurse specialist and all other involvement has ceased.

It is imperative that the client is prepared for the eventual withdrawal of intervention and support from the specialist nurse and other primary workers. One should bear in mind that it is just as detrimental to the successful outcome of therapeutic intervention to withdraw one's services too late, thus creating a dependency on oneself, as it is to withdraw from such interventions too early[1].

The preceding chapters represent the author's interpretation of the requirements for home detoxification. Others will have different opinions. It is suggested that one tries all reasonable approaches, adapting and perhaps even mixing them to suit one's own method of working, and of course to offer the best possible service to the client, family, and significant others.

At the present time, services are increasingly called upon to justify their existence. We must be able to account for the things we do and the interventions we offer, by evaluating our actions and making appropriate modifications to the benefit of those who use our services. The procedure and assessment process outlined in this book allow for research and subsequent evaluation which, one hopes, will lead to the development of more appropriate interventions for this client group.

It is nevertheless apparent that home detoxification has many advantages, in terms of cost and accessibility, over traditional inpatient methods. Stockwell *et al.*[2] suggest that detoxifications supervised at home by a community nurse could cost as little as 26% of specialist in-patient care. They point out that the community nurse in Exeter City supervised 36 detoxifications in 1990, which was equivalent to the total number of in-patient detoxifications for the combined Exeter mental health hospitals for the year prior to the project commencement in 1986.

As a result of ease of accessibility, home detoxification creates its own service demands, which in-patient care does not, and offers an improved, structured and active intervention facility for the problem drinker. Access to health service provision for all and the development of streamlined, cost-conscious health Trusts are currently active government targets; home detoxification fulfils these ideals. The introduction of this service provision in every health district is surely an essential and integral option for service managers.

Finally, whilst the aim of this book is to enhance knowledge and skill in the area of substance misuse intervention, and to inform professionals of appropriate procedures, merely having read it does not make one an 'expert'. Therefore, it is not intended to replace appropriate practical supervision and assessment of skills. This is essential until an acceptable level of practical competence and expertise has been achieved.

References

1. Cooper DB and Faugier J (1993) Substance misuse. In: Wright H and Giddy M (eds) *Mental health nursing: from first principles to professional practice.* Chapman and Hall, London.

2. Stockwell T, Bolt L, Milner I *et al.* (1991) Home detoxification from alcohol: its safety and efficiency in comparison with in-patient care. *Alcohol and Alcoholism,* **26** (5/6), 645–50.

Summary 1 The complete home detoxification procedure (HDP)

Note This procedure and the Guidelines for Assessing Suitability were established by the author in 1988. They are the cornerstones from which this book was developed, and have been widely applied.

It is suggested that service providers photocopy Summaries 1 and 2, and 'pin them up' in the practice/office for use as a practical step by step instruction or checklist.

The documentation referred to and forming an integral part of this procedure is described in detail in Chapter 3; a sample of each document/assessment tool follows (Appendices 1–13). The assessment tools have been designed specifically for use during home detoxification.

Home detoxification also involves a specific clinical procedure and should be undertaken by a qualified nurse who has undergone a period of training and supervision, and whose level of competence has been affirmed.

Definition of detoxification

For the purpose of this procedure, detoxification is 'a treatment designed to control both psychological and physiological complications which may occur temporarily after a period of heavy and sustained alcohol use'[1].

Source of referrals

An open referral system should be operated for home detoxification—ie from GPs, other professional and voluntary workers, the client, family, or significant others. If the referral is from a source other than the GP, then the latter must agree to medical involvement before home detoxification commences.

STAGE ONE Assessing suitability

Refer also to the guidelines in Summary 2.

A minority of clients are likely to experience distressing withdrawal symptoms on reduction, or cessation, of alcohol intake. A careful assessment should be conducted before commencing detoxification; a protocol for this is outlined below.

(i)   **Assessment of suitability.**
      Assessment for home detoxification should be conducted by a nurse specialist in alcohol misuse who has achieved a recognizable level of competence in this area of care.

(ii) **Supervision.**
      Supervision should be provided by a competent nurse specialist, who has appropriate teaching skills, to any nurse wishing to specialize in this procedure. Until such time as competency has been agreed, a case discussion should be held in each instance with the competent nurse specialist, prior to and during the detoxification process. The nurse specialist should also review client suitability and progress.

(iii) **Assessment interviews.**
      These should be undertaken within 24–48 hours of receiving the initial referral. Verbal telephone referrals will be accepted, but a fully completed referral form should follow by post. However, the non-receipt of a written request should not delay commencement of assessment or any subsequent treatment.

(iv) **The decision.**
      The decision to proceed with home detoxification rests solely with the nurse specialist who has agreed to supervise this process. It cannot be delegated.

(v)   **Initial assessment procedure.**
      This consists of answering two basic questions to determine whether the client needs supervised home detoxification.
      a) Is there a need to medicate for withdrawal symptoms? If YES:
      b) Are there any strong reasons for *not* keeping the client in the home environment whilst medication is administered?

(vi) **Establishing the need.**
      ▪ The client, having been fully informed, *must* express a clear wish to participate in home detoxification, and to cease alcohol consumption completely, at least for the duration of detoxi-

fication. The nurse specialist must *never* 'hard sell' this model of care.

■ If the client is very keen to stop, supervision may only be required if it seems likely that medication will be required to alleviate severe withdrawal symptoms.

STAGE TWO Taking a history

An assessment of recent, heavy and continuous alcohol and drug intake up to the day of assessment should be taken, using the following assessment documentation together with the guidelines in Summary 2.

(i) **Home detoxification initial assessment form (IAF)—Appendix 1.**
This contains a list of facts to check *prior* to commencement of home detoxification.

(ii) **Severity of alcohol dependence questionnaire (SADQ)—Appendix 2.**
This form should be completed by the client during the initial assessment procedure, and scored by the nurse specialist. The score ranges from 0–60.
The SADQ looks at a recent month of heavy drinking and is designed as a pure measure of the degree of alcohol dependence, focusing exclusively on the most readily quantifiable elements of the syndrome. The five areas assessed are:

■ physical withdrawal signs
■ affective withdrawal signs
■ withdrawal relief drinking
■ quantity and frequency of alcohol consumption
■ rapidity of onset of withdrawal symptoms following a period of abstinence.

Scores have a low but significant correlation with severity of withdrawal for individuals. Scores of –30 indicate mild to moderate dependence/severity; scores of 30+ indicate severe dependence/severity.

Home detoxification should not be commenced unless it has been discussed with the GP.

(iii)   **Problems inventory (PI)—Appendix 3**
This should be completed by the client. It assists in the assessment of the level of problems incurred as a result of excessive alcohol consumption.

(iv)   **Home environment assessment—Appendix 13**
This is designed to assess suitability for detoxification within the home, and is completed by the nurse specialist.

STAGE THREE   Procedure following acceptance

If assessment indicates suitability for home detoxification, the nurse specialist must then:

(i)   check that the GP is willing to accept medical responsibility. If appropriate, an appointment should be made for the client to see the GP

(ii)   describe the home detoxification procedure to the client and the family, and give them an information leaflet (Appendix 4, page 104)

(iii)   request permission to take blood samples for a liver function test (LFT), full blood count (FBC) and blood alcohol concentration (BAC)—paying particular attention to the results of gamma GT, ALT, AST, MCV and bilirubin. Blood tests should be taken as required and at a later follow-up as agreed. The results should be returned to the GP records after recording in the IAF.
        [Note   Each nurse specialist must have attended and qualified from an approved venepuncture training course before undertaking this procedure within the client's home.]

(iv)   discuss the medication regime and agree boundaries with the GP, client, and family

(v)   arrange for the client or family to collect the prescribed medication

(vi)   agree with the client and family the contents of the consent and contract forms (Appendices 6 and 7, pages 109 and 111). These should be signed once the level of commitment has been fully explained.

STAGE FOUR   On commencement of home detoxification

The nurse who is conducting the detoxification should:

(i)   complete the checklist on the IAF and ensure all information is up to date

(ii)   enter symptom severity checklist (SSC) daily record (Appendices 8 and 9, pages 113 and 115) first results in the IAF. All subsequent results should be recorded in the continuing assessment form (CAF) (Appendix 10, page 116). The SSC is a means of monitoring daily withdrawal symptoms. Each question is rated 0–3; if a total score of 18+ is indicated, the GP should be contacted *before* proceeding

(iii)   take a breathalyzer reading and record it on the IAF. This must be done in a low key and relaxed fashion. It is undertaken for safety reasons and assists in ensuring effectiveness of the detoxification procedure

(iv)   take blood samples as outlined on page 88. The results should be recorded in the IAF, and then forwarded to the GP

(v)   take, and record on the IAF, the pulse, temperature and blood pressure. If these are very high or very low, the nurse should consult the GP *before* proceeding

(vi)   advise on medication, including dose, route, frequency, side-effects and contraindications. If the family or a friend cannot hold the medication, the nurse should take charge of the drugs until detoxification is completed

(vii)   discuss relapse and relapse management with the client

(viii) advise on method of contact in an emergency or crisis

(ix)   if all the above are satisfactory, commence detoxification.

STAGE FIVE   Procedure for subsequent/daily visits

(i)   Monitor for signs of under- or over-sedation, such as a rapid fall in blood pressure. Consult with the GP if you are concerned.

(ii)   Complete the SSC daily and record the results on the CAF (Appendix 10, page 116). Report any concerns to the GP before proceeding.

(iii)   Take breathalyzer, pulse, temperature and blood pressure readings, and record them on the CAF.

(iv) Review the prescribed medication and administer as required. The nurse specialist should decide whether medication needs to be altered—ie decreased, increased or discontinued—following full discussion with the client, family and GP.

(v) Advise, counsel, reassure and support the client and family. Discuss future plans and the programme at each visit.

(vi) If it is not possible for the nurse specialist to undertake post-detoxification counselling/support, a primary worker or counsellor should be introduced to the client and family at the first opportunity. Joint visits should be made *before* detoxification is completed.

(vii) All the above information, and a visit summary, should be recorded on the CAF. This also incorporates the daily SSC. Number the forms to correspond with each day of detoxification, eg day 1, 2, 3, etc.

(viii) If all the results remain within normal limits, proceed with detoxification.

STAGE SIX   At the end of detoxification

(i) Request that the client and the family complete the satisfaction scales (Appendices 11 and 12, pages 119 and 121). These facilitate evaluation of the home detoxification procedure and will assist in the enhancement of service provision in the future.

(ii) Review plans and the programme. Discuss relapse management and give a contact point in case of emergency/crisis.

STAGE SEVEN   Follow-up assessment

Confirm the three month, one year and five year follow-up dates and reaffirm consent. Enter records in a log book or computer for further action. Such follow-up arrangements facilitate long-term evaluation of the service and are an essential component of the research process. Nursing is a research-led profession and every nurse specialist must actively participate in this process if service evaluation and development are to be effective.

Reference

1. Stockwell T (1987) The Exeter home detoxification project. In: Stockwell T and Clement S (eds) *Helping the problem drinker: a new initiative in community care*. Croom Helm, London.

Summary 2 Guidelines for assessing suitability for home detoxification

STAGE ONE   Establishing the need

Most clients with drink related problems can stop, or reduce, their alcohol intake without any medication for withdrawal symptoms. Some may have already done so by the time you see them. However, a few individuals experience symptoms severe enough to make it necessary, and appropriate, that medication is given to assist in the detoxification process.

Therefore, we must ask, 'Is it possible to estimate the likely severity of alcohol withdrawal in an individual?' and 'Is medication required to assist in this process?'. Some methods for finding the answers to these questions are given below.

(i)   **Recent regular and heavy alcohol/drug use and misuse.**
Even one week of continuous, heavy alcohol consumption can result in distressing withdrawal symptoms. However, medication is not usually required to assist alcohol withdrawal for women who drink less than 12 units of alcohol per day, or men who drink less than 16 units per day.

It is important to take a full alcohol and drug history prior to making the decision to commence home detoxification. Beware of the client who combines alcohol and tranquillizer use, or who combines alcohol with depressant drugs; the symptoms will be more severe.

(ii)   **Recent experience of withdrawal symptoms.**
Always enquire about alcohol withdrawal experiences during previous attempts to control or stop drinking—eg the shakes, panic, anxiety, withdrawal fits—and following a period of temporary abstinence (eg on waking) when the BAC is at its lowest. Question the client about early morning relief drinking. This information will give an indication of the potential severity of alcohol withdrawal and appropriate interventions required to assist the client through this process.

The severity of alcohol dependence questionnaire (SADQ) is a useful assessment tool. The first three sections, in particular, should be used in all cases before deciding on home detoxification.

STAGE TWO   Assessing the risk

If it appears that the client needs supervised detoxification, and he or she is well motivated, it is important to make further checks for suitability by considering the following factors.

(i)   **Previous withdrawal problems.**
Clients who, on several occasions, fail to complete detoxification at home, and those who experience withdrawal fits, are 'high risk' individuals: they usually require hospital admission. Clients who take anti-depressant drugs or tranquillizers will also need special consideration; such drugs can lower the 'fit threshold', thus exacerbating the risks attached to home detoxification. However, these effects can be overcome by increasing medication, and this option should be fully investigated.

(ii)   **Home environment.**
- The home environment should be relatively stable. The client with no fixed abode (NFA), or who lives in accommodation with a high turnover of residents (eg a night shelter), may not be suitable.
- Too many people living in the home may cause problems. Look for overcrowding and a high noise level, and observe whether other residents or the family are sympathetic: will they adjust their behaviour accordingly?
- Assess alcohol and drug use or misuse by other occupants: access to alcohol should be kept to a minimum. If this is not possible (eg in the case of a licensee wishing to undergo home detoxification) special care is needed to ensure that the client has an adequate support network.
- Boisterous young (under school age) children, inconsiderate children or teenagers may be a problem, especially if living conditions are cramped.
- A minimum degree of support must be available, although not necessarily within the home. It will help the client to know support is quickly and readily available.

(iii)   **Psychological state.**
The client who is a suicide risk, or who has intentionally overdosed (especially during alcohol withdrawal) in the past,

demands hospital admission. Signs of serious mental health problems suggest that the client needs hospital care.

(iv) **Physical state.**

There are two things to look for in this category:

- First, it is important to establish the client's nutritional status. An individual who has been reliant on alcohol as the major source of nutrition for a month or more is at risk, and hospital admission may be indicated. In such circumstances, the likelihood of both brain and liver damage increases, and sudden cessation of alcohol can cause serious problems unless appropriate vitamin replacement is given. Even if the client returns to a balanced diet during detoxification (which is unlikely in the early stages), this is insufficient to satisfy the body's need in such circumstances.
- Second, if there is an underlying serious medical condition, hospitalization may be more appropriate. Always check with the GP about possible physiological (and psychological) complications.

Appendix 1 Home detoxification initial assessment form (IAF)

Name . . . . Date . . . .

Partner/friend name . . . . Code number . . . .

Relationship to client . . . . Referral date . . . .

Referral agent . . . . GP . . . .

DOB . . . . Hospital number . . . . . .

Checklist (tick)

- GP assessment of suitability and agreed involvement. ☐
- Physical examination and blood tests. ☐
- Medication prescribed. ☐
- Support of family or friend. ☐
- Client and supporter fact sheet given. ☐
- Contact name and number given. ☐
- Contract/consent form signed—client and supporter. ☐
- GP informed of commencement and client consent. ☐
- Check if alcohol or drugs on the premises. ☐
- Nurse specialist drug administration record completed. ☐

History of withdrawal symptoms (please print)

Present circumstances (please print)

Time of assessment . . . . am/pm

Blood pressure . . . . . . Pulse . . . . . Breathalyzer reading . . . . .

Temperature . . . . Home environment assessment (HEA) score . . .

Symptom severity checklist (SSC) score . . . .

SSC client version score . . . .

Blood results:
Gamma GT . . . . (M=10–48 iu/l F=8–28 iu/l)

ALT . . . . (5–30 iu/l)   AST . . . . (10–40 iu/l)

MCV . . . . (80–96 fl)   BAC . . . . mg/100 ml (0)

Bilirubin . . . .

Other significant results from LFT and FBC . . . .

SADQ results:
Mild/moderate dependency . . . –30   Severe dependency . . . 30+

Summary of home assessment   Problems identified by the client
or family, etc. (please print)

Date and time of next visit . . . .

Signed . . . . , Nurse Specialist   Date . . . .

Agreed drugs dosage over detoxification period:

1 Drug . . . . . . Dose . . . . . . Frequency . . . . . . Route . . . . . .

2 Drug . . . . . . Dose . . . . . . Frequency . . . . . . Route . . . . . .

3 Drug . . . . . . Dose . . . . . . Frequency . . . . . . Route . . . . . .

4 Drug . . . . . . Dose . . . . . . Frequency . . . . . . Route . . . . . .

Day	Date	Drug given	Time	Signed
1				
2				
3				
4				
5				
6				
7				
8				
9				

Appendix 2 Severity of alcohol dependence questionnaire (SADQ)

Please answer all questions

We would like you to recall a recent month when you were drinking in a way which, for you, was fairly typical of a heavy drinking period. Please fill in the month and the year. Month . . . . . Year . . . . .

We would like to know more about your drinking during this time and during other periods when your drinking experience was similar. We want to know how often you experienced certain feelings. Please reply to each statement by putting a **circle** round **Almost Never** or **Sometimes** or **Often** or **Nearly Always** after each question.

Please indicate below the physical symptoms that you have experienced **first thing in the morning** during typical periods of heavy drinking.

1 I wake up feeling sweaty.

Almost Never	Sometimes	Often	Nearly Always
0	1	2	3

2 My hands shake first thing in the morning.

Almost Never	Sometimes	Often	Nearly Always
0	1	2	3

3 My whole body shakes violently first thing in the morning if I don't have a drink.

Almost Never	Sometimes	Often	Nearly Always
0	1	2	3

4 I wake up absolutely drenched in sweat.

Almost Never	Sometimes	Often	Nearly Always
0	1	2	3

The following statements refer to moods and states of mind you may have experienced **first thing in the morning** during these periods of heavy drinking.

5 I dread waking up in the morning.

Almost Never	Sometimes	Often	Nearly Always
0	1	2	3

6 I am frightened of meeting people first thing in the morning.

Almost Never	Sometimes	Often	Nearly Always
0	1	2	3

7 I feel at the edge of despair when I first wake up.

Almost Never	Sometimes	Often	Nearly Always
0	1	2	3

8 I feel very frightened when I wake up.

Almost Never	Sometimes	Often	Nearly Always
0	1	2	3

The following statements refer to morning drinking habits during the recent period when you were drinking heavily, and periods like it.

9 I like to have a morning drink.

Almost Never	Sometimes	Often	Nearly Always
0	1	2	3

10 I always gulp my first few morning drinks down as quickly as possible.

Almost Never	Sometimes	Often	Nearly Always
0	1	2	3

11 I drink in the morning to get rid of the shakes.

Almost Never	Sometimes	Often	Nearly Always
0	1	2	3

12 I have a very strong craving for a drink when I wake up.

Almost Never	Sometimes	Often	Nearly Always
0	1	2	3

The following statements refer to degree of alcohol consumption during the recent period of heavy drinking and periods like it.

13 I drink more than a quarter of a bottle of spirits per day (4 doubles *or* 1 bottle of wine *or* 4 pints of beer/lager).

Almost Never	Sometimes	Often	Nearly Always
0	1	2	3

14 I drink more than half a bottle of spirits per day (*or* 2 bottles of wine *or* 8 pints of beer/lager).

Almost Never	Sometimes	Often	Nearly Always
0	1	2	3

15 I drink more than one bottle of spirits per day (*or* 4 bottles of wine *or* 15 pints of beer/lager).

Almost Never	Sometimes	Often	Nearly Always
0	1	2	3

16 I drink more than two bottles of spirits per day (*or* 8 bottles of wine *or* 30 pints of beer/lager).

Almost Never	Sometimes	Often	Nearly Always
0	1	2	3

Imagine the following situation:

(a) You have been **completely off drink** for a few weeks.
(b) You then drink **very heavily for two days.**

How would you feel the **morning after** those two days of heavy drinking?

17 I would start to sweat.

Not at all	Slightly	Moderately	Quite a lot
0	1	2	3

18 My hands would shake.

Not at all	Slightly	Moderately	Quite a lot
0	1	2	3

19 My body would shake.

Not at all	Slightly	Moderately	Quite a lot
0	1	2	3

20 I would be craving for a drink.

Not at all	Slightly	Moderately	Quite a lot
0	1	2	3

Thank you for completing this form

TOTAL SCORE: . . . . . .

(A score of −30 indicates mild to moderate dependence. 30+ indicates severe dependence.)

Appendix 3 Problems inventory (PI)

Name .... Date ....

Code number ....

We would like to ask you several routine questions, some of which may strike you as odd or embarrassing, but we hope you will feel able to answer.

In the past two months: (CIRCLE as appropriate)

1 Have you lost touch with a good friend due to your drinking? — YES/NO

2 Has your spouse or partner threatened to leave you because of your drinking? — YES/NO

3 Have you had arguments with close friends or relatives about your drinking? — YES/NO

4 Have you had an accident while drinking, resulting in injury to yourself needing medical attention and/or time off work? — YES/NO

5 Have you had an accident while drinking, resulting in damage to property to the value of £50 or more? — YES/NO

6 Have you been admitted to hospital because of your drinking, or because of some harm it has caused? — YES/NO

7 Have you lost a job as a result of your drinking? — YES/NO

8 Have you been warned about poor performance, or behaviour, at work? — YES/NO

9 Have you missed whole days from work, or half days, regularly (at least once a week) due to your drinking? — YES/NO

10 Have you sold your own, or your family's, possessions, in order to buy alcohol? — YES/NO

11 Have you got into trouble, being violent or aggres-   YES/NO
    sive (while drinking), so that neighbours or the pol-
    ice were called in?

12 Have you been asked to leave someone's home, a   YES/NO
    public house or some other public place because of
    your drunken behaviour?

13 Have you stolen in order to get alcohol?   YES/NO

14 Have you been convicted of drunk driving?   YES/NO

15 Have you been convicted for being drunk and   YES/NO
    disorderly?

16 Have you passed out while drinking (not just   YES/NO
    fallen asleep at home)?

17 Have you had 'blackouts' or prolonged memory   YES/NO
    losses during a drinking session?

Thank you for completing this form

Appendix 4 Information about alcohol withdrawal for the partner or friend of the problem drinker

During home detoxification, it is helpful if the person undergoing treatment is offered support by a partner or friend. I shall visit regularly at agreed times during this period, to supervise the detoxification and to support you in your role. If you have any concerns or queries, please feel free to discuss these during my visit, or by contacting me on the telephone number given below.

During alcohol withdrawal, attention and care must be given and you can actively and safely participate as follows.

Safety

Your partner/friend may feel tremulous or drowsy, especially in the early stages of detoxification. Therefore, it is important to make the home environment as safe as possible: supervise smoking, don't allow the person to pour hot water, and avoid swimming, unsupervised bathing, driving or operating machinery.

Hygiene

It is possible that your partner/friend may sweat excessively. This is not unusual. Assistance with washing or bathing may be helpful if difficulty is experienced.

Environment

During alcohol withdrawal, the nervous system occasionally gets overexcited; your partner/friend may complain of extreme sensitivity to his or her surroundings (eg light, noises). He or she may also complain of feeling anxious and may appear irritable. Try to keep the home surroundings as calm, relaxing and quiet as possible. Tell me if you think these problems are getting worse.

Psychology

If your partner/friend complains of feeling anxious or fearful, or is unable to sleep, try to act in a reassuring manner and avoid unnecessary demands or stresses. Allow plenty of rest, especially in the first few days. However, if possible discourage too much 'napping' during the day as this may prevent the person from sleeping at night. Sometimes withdrawal symptoms are worse at night. Your partner/friend may find it helpful if a light is kept on in the bedroom.

Hydration

In cases of excessive sweating and/or vomiting in the early stages of withdrawal, it is important that your partner/friend drinks plenty of fluids. Orange juice may irritate the stomach and cause nausea. Milk is better as it eases digestive problems and, of course, water is an excellent thirst quencher. Sweet drinks, such as sweet tea or coffee, should be encouraged to prevent the blood sugar from falling too low.

Eating

Encourage small meals if possible (little and often), but don't worry if this is not possible in the first few days. The injections/tablets that I give will help replace any lost vitamins. It is best to offer a diet rich in protein (eg fish, dairy products and vegetables) and vitamins (eg cereals, nuts, pulses, milk, cheese, liver, poultry, citrus fruits, tomatoes and potatoes).

Drugs

A tranquillizer drug may have been prescribed to increase safety and comfort during the withdrawal period. As with all drugs, this is potentially addictive; it is therefore important that the correct dose is given and only for a limited number of days, (approximately 7–9 days). I will explain to you separately about any side-effects to look out for. It is important that you agree to take responsibility for any medication; holding it and giving it as prescribed. If you feel unable to do this, then it is possible for me to maintain control of the drug.

We will provide you with a booklet in which to record all the drugs taken, the dose, the time and any side-effects.

Note   If any symptoms persist, or appear to worsen, do not hesitate to contact me or your GP for advice.

Withdrawal fits

Very rarely (one in 100 people undergoing detoxification), withdrawal fits may occur. In the unlikely event of this happening, it is important that you follow a few simple rules.

When a person is having a fit, the initial stage visible to you will be the collapse and shaking/twitching of the limbs and torso. This may appear dramatic and frightening, but do not be tempted to intervene at this stage. You will be of more help to your partner/friend if you move any obstacles out of the way to prevent injury. This stage may last for a few seconds or a few minutes. During this time, the person may appear to stop breathing, and may go blue in the face and hands; this is perfectly natural and the normal colour will be regained when the fit stops. If the fit continues for longer than a few minutes, or stops and starts in rapid succession, or you feel worried, call your GP or an emergency ambulance on the 999 number *immediately*. In the majority of cases there is a full and quick recovery, with no long-term ill effects. Here are a few 'dos' and 'don'ts' to help you:

- *Don't* try to restrict the person when he or she is having the fit.
- *Don't* put, or force, anything into the mouth when the person is having the fit. By doing so, you may cause damage to the teeth and mouth, and possibly damage to your hands.
- *Do* remove any obstacles which the person may knock his- or herself on.
- After the fit has stopped, *do* check the mouth and make sure the airway is clear. If there are any obstructions, remove them.
- *Do* time the fit if possible.
- When the person has stopped 'fitting' he or she will go into a semi-conscious state. This is perfectly natural. *Do* ensure that breathing is normal; then lie the person on one side in a semi-prone position. I will explain how to do this if you are unsure. Ensure that the mouth is clear of any obstructions and place the head in such a way as to allow any fluids, or vomit, to run freely out without

being inhaled. For a short time after waking, the person may appear irritable and/or confused/disorientated. This is natural and will not last.

- *Do* allow the person time to come round completely; then make him or her comfortable and explain what has happened.
- Loss of muscle control during the fit may have caused incontinence which will be embarrassing for your partner. *Do* reassure that this is alright and natural. As soon as your partner/friend feels able, assist a change into comfortable dry clothing.
- *Do* ring me or the GP on the contact number below.

The process of stopping drinking and staying stopped can be a difficult one, for the drinker and also for the partner/friend and family. In addition to my role during detoxification, I will be available to give further support, advice or counselling at any future time. *Never* be afraid to ask.

My name is . . . .

My contact number is . . . .

Appendix 5 Medication monitoring booklet (held by partner/friend)

Day	Date	Drug given and dose	Time	Side-effects
1				
2				
3				
4				
5				
6				
7				
8				
9				

Appendix 6 Contract and consent form for home detoxification—client

Please read, sign and date this form as confirmation that the home detoxification procedure has been explained to you, and that you wish to undergo detoxification at home and will comply with the following conditions.

- You will not drink alcohol during the agreed period of detoxification, and you will comply with requests for regular breathalyzer testing.
- You will take all medication as prescribed and agreed with you, your partner/friend, your GP and the nurse specialist supervising the detoxification.
- Should you recommence drinking, you will, on request, hand over all prescribed medication to the supervising nurse specialist.
- You will allow the nurse specialist to visit your home as arranged, to supervise the detoxification and check your medical and psychological condition.
- You agree to blood tests prior to detoxification and at all other times felt to be clinically necessary, including each follow-up occasion. The reason for these tests has been fully explained and is understood. The results of all blood tests will be recorded on your file and the originals forwarded to your GP.
- You agree to the use of your blood test results for the purposes of a research project, provided full confidentiality is ensured. This research has been fully explained to you.
- You will agree to follow-up interviews at three months, one year and five years in addition to any other agreed care, for the purposes of the previously explained research. The dates have been agreed as:

Three months: . . . .

One year: . . . .

Five years: . . . .

Signed . . . .

Date . . . .

Signed . . . . , Nurse Specialist

Date . . . .

Note Withholding consent to follow-up assessments, or for the use of data for research purposes, will *not* exclude you from home detoxification. All information held by us is strictly confidential and you will not be identifiable to any other person except the nurse specialist involved with your care.

Appendix 7 Contract and consent form for home detoxification—partner or friend

Please sign below if you agree to the following conditions, and to confirm that they have been fully explained to you and relate to this home detoxification and the research project being undertaken to evaluate the effectiveness of such a service provision.

- You have read and understand the information provided about alcohol withdrawal.
- You are/are not (delete as appropriate) willing to take responsibility for the prescribed medication, and you understand that the usual prescription charges will be made.
- Should the person resume drinking, you will inform the nurse specialist and will return all prescribed medication to him or her immediately.
- You will keep and maintain the daily record of medication and monitor any side-effects, reporting any concerns to the nurse specialist and/or GP.
- You are willing to be interviewed, for the purposes of research, as has been explained to you. This will be at three month, one year, and five year intervals. The dates for these interviews have been agreed as:

Three months: . . . .

One year: . . . .

Five years: . . . .

Signed . . . .

Date . . . .

Signed . . . . , Nurse Specialist

Date . . . .

Note Withholding consent to follow-up assessments, or for the use of data for research purposes, will *not* exclude your partner/friend from home detoxification. All information held by us is strictly confidential and you will not be identifiable to any other person except the nurse specialist involved with your care.

Appendix 8 Symptom severity checklist (SSC)

Name . . . . Date . . . .

Code number . . . .

Please CIRCLE *one* number in each case.

ORIENTATION
0   fully orientated
1   mildly disorientated
2   obviously disorientated
3   totally disorientated

LEVEL OF
CONSCIOUSNESS
0   fully alert
1   slightly drowsy
2   very drowsy
3   roused with difficulty

HALLUCINATIONS
0   no hallucinations
1   unstructured
2   intermittent structured
3   frequent structured

AGITATION
0   no sign of agitation
1   slight restlessness
2   moderate restlessness
3   constantly restless

MOOD
0   cheerful/appropriate
1   sometimes low
2   often low
3   despondent

ANXIETY
0   finds it easy to relax
1   finds it difficult to relax
2   hardly ever relaxed
3   cannot relax

SLEEP
0   sleeps well
1   broken sleep
2   difficulty in getting to sleep
3   insomnia

APPETITE
0   good appetite
1   fair appetite
2   poor appetite
3   no appetite

SWEATING

0   no sweating
1   slight
2   moderate
3   profuse

GI DISTURBANCE

0   no abnormalities
1   mild nausea
2   persistent nausea
3   vomiting, two or more
    times

TREMOR

0   none
1   slight
2   moderate
3   marked

COMMITMENT TO DETOX

0   strong
1   moderate
2   slight
3   none

CONVULSIONS

YES/NO. If yes, how many and duration . . . .

OTHER SYMPTOMS

YES/NO. If yes, what? . . . .

. . . .

. . . .

TOTAL SCORE: . . . . (A score of 18+ indicates
concern—consult the GP)

Appendix 9 The client's daily SSC rating

Name . . . . Date . . . .

Day number . . . .

CRAVING

My present desire for a drink is:

0   not at all
1   mild
2   moderate
3   strong
4   very strong

ANXIETY

0   easy to relax
1   difficult to relax
2   hardly ever fully relaxed
3   cannot sit still for long

SLEEP DISTURBANCE

0   slept well
1   sleep was broken
2   total insomnia

CLIENT SCORE: . . . .

Appendix 10 Home detoxification continuing assessment form (CAF)

Day number ...... Visit number .... Code number ....

Name .... Hospital number ......

Symptom severity checklist—Please CIRCLE *one* number in each case.

ORIENTATION
0   fully orientated
1   mildly disorientated
2   obviously disorientated
3   totally disorientated

LEVEL OF
CONSCIOUSNESS
0   fully alert
1   slightly drowsy
2   very drowsy
3   roused with difficulty

HALLUCINATIONS
0   no hallucinations
1   unstructured
2   intermittent structured
3   frequent structured

AGITATION
0   no sign of agitation
1   slight restlessness
2   moderate restlessness
3   constantly restless

MOOD
0   cheerful/appropriate
1   sometimes low
2   often low
3   despondent

ANXIETY
0   finds it easy to relax
1   finds it difficult to relax
2   hardly ever relaxed
3   cannot relax

SLEEP
0   sleeps well
1   broken sleep
2   difficulty in getting to sleep
3   insomnia

APPETITE
0   good appetite
1   fair appetite
2   poor appetite
3   no appetite

SWEATING

0   no sweating
1   slight
2   moderate
3   profuse

GI DISTURBANCE

0   no abnormalities
1   mild nausea
2   persistent nausea
3   vomiting, two or more times

TREMOR

0   none
1   slight
2   moderate
3   marked

COMMITMENT TO DETOX

0   strong
1   moderate
2   slight
3   none

CONVULSIONS:

YES/NO. If yes, how many and duration . . . .

OTHER SYMPTOMS:

YES/NO. If yes, what? . . . .

. . . .

. . . .

TOTAL SCORE: . . . . . (A score of 18+ indicates concern—consult the GP)

Time . . . . . . am/pm   Blood pressure . . . . Pulse . . . .

Breathalyzer . . . . . .

a)   SSC score . . . . Temperature . . . .

b)   Client SSC score . . . .

Blood test results (if applicable)

Gamma GT . . . . . . ALT . . . . AST . . . .

MCV . . . . BAC . . . . Bilirubin . . . .

Other significant results from: FBC . . . .

                                        LFT . . . .

Medication prescribed over next 24 hours (if different from present agreement)

Summary of visit (include problems identified during the last 24 hours)

Date and time of next visit . . . .

Signed . . . . , Nurse Specialist   Date . . . .

Appendix 11 Confidential client satisfaction scale

Date . . . . Code number . . . .

Interviewer's name . . . .

The questions are designed to help us evaluate the detoxification procedure and its effectiveness. Please place an 'X' on each of the lines provided to show how you felt.

Please answer every question

1 On the whole, how did you feel during your withdrawal from alcohol?

Very comfortable	├───────────────┤	Very uncomfortable
Well supported	├───────────────┤	Not well supported
Not craving for alcohol	├───────────────┤	Craving for alcohol
Very calm	├───────────────┤	Very anxious
In control of yourself	├───────────────┤	Controlled by others
Very determined	├───────────────┤	Not at all determined
Not at all tempted	├───────────────┤	Very tempted to drink
Well informed	├───────────────┤	Not at all well informed

2   Was the medication:

Too much |—————————————————| Too little

Too long |—————————————————| Too short

3   Were the visits from the nurse specialist:

Too |—————————————————| Not frequent
frequent   enough

4   During the home detoxification, how helpful were the following:

a) support from your partner or friend

Unhelpful |—————————————————| Vital

b) support from the nurse specialist

Unhelpful |—————————————————| Vital

c) support from other agencies (state) . . . .

Unhelpful |—————————————————| Vital

d) support from your GP

Unhelpful |—————————————————| Vital

e) visits by the nurse specialist

Unhelpful |—————————————————| Vital

f) drugs prescribed by your GP

Unhelpful |—————————————————| Vital

g) the physical check-up

Unhelpful |—————————————————| Vital

h) the breathalyzer

Unhelpful |—————————————————| Vital

5   What did you like the most, or find most helpful about the home detoxification procedure?

6   What did you like the least, or find least helpful about the home detoxification procedure?

Thank you for completing this form.
Please check that you have answered all the questions.

Appendix 12 Confidential supporter satisfaction scale

Date .... Code number ....

Interviewer's name ....

The questions below are designed to help us evaluate the detoxification procedure and its effectiveness. Please place an 'X' on each of the lines provided to show how you felt.

Please answer every question

1 On the whole, how did you feel being involved in this home detoxification?

Very confident	⊢——————————⊣	Not at all confident
Well supported	⊢——————————⊣	Not well supported
Well informed	⊢——————————⊣	Not well informed
Very calm	⊢——————————⊣	Very anxious
In control	⊢——————————⊣	Not in control

2 Were the visits from the nurse specialist:

| Too frequent | ⊢——————————⊣ | Not frequent enough |

3 During home detoxification, how helpful were the following:
a) the information sheet for relatives and friends

| Unhelpful | ⊢——————————⊣ | Vital |

b) support from the nurse specialist

| Unhelpful | ⊢——————————⊣ | Vital |

c) support from the GP

Unhelpful |————————————| Vital

d) the visit from the nurse specialist

Unhelpful |————————————| Vital

e) drugs prescribed by the GP

Unhelpful |————————————| Vital

f) the breathalyzer checks

Unhelpful |————————————| Vital

g) having a telephone number for immediate advice

Unhelpful |————————————| Vital

4   What did you find helped you the most during this home detoxification?

5   What did you find least helpful during this home detoxification?

Thank you for completing this form.
Please check that you have answered every question.

Appendix 13 Home environment assessment (HEA)

AVAILABILITY OF
SUPPORTER

0 always available
1 often available
2 sometimes available
3 never available

ATTITUDE OF
SUPPORTER

0 very supportive
1 supportive
2 slightly supportive
3 not supportive

COMMITMENT OF
SUPPORTER

0 very committed
1 committed
2 slightly committed
3 not committed

LEVEL
OF NOISE

0 tranquil
1 reasonably quiet
2 noisy
3 very noisy

SPACE TO
BE ALONE

0 ample room
1 some room
2 little room
3 none

PRESENCE OF YOUNG
CHILDREN AND/OR PETS

0 no children or pets
1 sometimes present
2 always present
3 presence is disruptive

GENERAL
ATMOSPHERE

0 very organized
1 organized
2 slightly disorganized
3 disorganized

PRESENCE OF OTHER
DRINKERS

0 never present
1 sometimes present
2 often present
3 always present

HEA SCORE: . . . .

Will the client be living at home address   1—YES   2—NO
for 4 week period?

If working, will client continue to work   1—YES   2—NO
during detoxification?

HEA SCORE: . . . .

Comments . . . .

. . . .

Appendices references

1. Bennie C (1991) Home detoxification service for problem drinkers. Report for Forth Valley Health Authority (personal communication). (Appendix 13)

2. Cooper DB (1992) *Home detoxification policy and procedures.* 2nd Edition. North East Essex Health Authority.

3. Murphy DJ, Shaw GK and Clark I (1983) Tiapride and chlormethiazole in alcohol withdrawal: a double-blind trial. *Alcohol and Alcoholism*, 18 (3), 227–37. (Appendices 8 & 9)

4. Stockwell T, Bolt L, Milner I *et al.* (1990) Home detoxification for problem drinkers: acceptability to clients, relatives, general practitioners and outcome after 60 days. *British Journal of Addiction*, 85 (1), 61–70. (Appendices 3, 11 & 12)

5. Stockwell T, Murphy D and Hodgson R (1983) The severity of alcohol dependence questionnaire: its use, reliability and validity. *British Journal of Addiction*, 78 (2), 145–55. (Appendix 2)

Recommended reading

Davidson R, Rollnick S and MacEwan I (eds) (1991) *Counselling problem drinkers*. Routledge, London.

Heather N and Robertson I (1983) *Controlled drinking*. Cambridge University Press, Cambridge.

Hobson R (1989) *Forms of feeling: the heart of psychotherapy*. Routledge, London.

Kennedy J and Faugier J (1989) *Drugs and alcohol dependency nursing*. Heinemann Nursing, Oxford.

McMahon R and Pearson A (1992) *Nursing as therapy*. Chapman and Hall, London.

Miller WR and Heather N (eds) (1986) *Treating addictive behaviours: process of change*. Plenum, London.

Miller WR and Rollnick S (1991) *Motivational interviewing: preparing people to change addictive behaviour*. Guilford Press, New York.

Nelson-Jones R (1992) *Practical counselling skills*. 2nd Edition. Cassell, London.

Wright H and Giddey M (1993) *Mental health nursing: from first principles to professional practice*. Chapman and Hall, London.

Index